BRIDGE DONOR

THE JOURNEY OF A LIVING ORGAN DONOR

KELLY C. BERWAGER PH.D.

Copyright © 2018 by Kelly C Berwager Ph.D.

Cover Design – Nic Monroe & Adam Davis

Editor – Danielle Wallace

Book Formatting & Layout– Adam Davis

All rights reserved.

ISBN (Print): 13-978-09994938-8-5

ISBN (eBook): 13-978-0-9994938-9-2

CONTENTS

Dedication   ix

Introduction   xix

January   1

February   7

March   25

April   35

May   43

June   50

July   65

August   78

September   96

October   110

November   121

December   130

The Rest Of The Story   165

About the Author   205

ENDORSEMENTS

In *Bridge Donor*, Kelly Berwager takes you with her on a journey to make one of the biggest, most selfless decisions of her life: becoming a living organ donor. Her story is deeply encouraging and light-hearted. This book can help others understand how to hear from God, how to surrender, and how to follow His voice.

— -Karol Hobbs, Executive Assistant to Chris Hodges, Church of the Highlands, Birmingham, AL

Kelly's story is an incredible testimony of what being submitted to God is all about. It is a story of obedience and sacrifice that not only saved one life but will inspire countless others!

— -Doug Hall, Dream Team, Church of the Highlands, Birmingham, AL

At the core, Kelly Berwager puts into prose a message of faith, hope, and love. A life's work and journey that manifests itself in the most incredible gift one can give - the gift of life. It is a message that transcends all that is wrong in the world and reminds you of the goodness in each of us.

— -Dr. Jayme Locke, MD, MPH
Director, CTI Outcomes Research
Center; Director, Incompatible
Kidney & KPD Program; Director
Transplant Analytics, Informatics
& Quality-University of Alabama
at Birmingham; Birmingham, AL

It was an honor and a pleasure to read about this spiritual experience. Dr. Berwager's personality shines through in every line of this very personal narrative and it is a blessing to see the growth, challenges, and the sheer amount of faith that inspired her to follow Gods' plan.

— -Kirsten B. Jones, Art Education
Student, Troy University, Troy, AL

DEDICATION

*"The LORD gave me this answer: "Write
down clearly on tablets what I reveal to
you, so that it can be read at a glance."*

— Habakkuk 2:2 (GNT)

As cliché as it sounds, this book really was a labor of love. Although it feels like it took way too long to complete such a short book, it has been an emotional journey I am proud to see completed.

Writing about the events of 2014 was both emotionally draining and spiritually exhilarating. I thought knowing the end of the story would make writing this book an easier task, but it didn't.

Reliving every event, every moment, every feeling of that year took me back to the people, places, and prayers that contributed to this story of listening to God direct every facet of my life and realizing I am not in control of life like I once thought I was.

Living through the events of 2014 taught me many things about myself, the love of family and friends, and the power of God's grace. I learned I can do just about anything IF, and this is a big "if", I seek God's direction, listen intently to His guidance, and follow the path He lays out for me. I learned family can be our biggest champions and drive us crazy in the process, all while loving us unconditionally. I learned friends can also be our biggest advocates and cheerleaders, while also holding our feet to the fire by questioning us when we need to stop and reevaluate a situation.

The biggest lesson I learned throughout 2014 and beyond came from God himself. He taught me that He can take any person or any situation and use it for good. People and their situations can be used to glorify God and His amazing grace, IF they're willing to listen and see Him in every aspect of our lives. He's talking to us all the time, but it's our choice to listen and trust. And that's just what I did in 2014 and now try to do on a daily basis.

By allowing God to take my seemingly mundane life and serve Him through the donation of one of my kidneys has taught me more about loving others than any other event in my life. I've grown as a child of God, a wife, a mother, a daughter, a sister, a teacher, and a friend. I am eternally thankful for the experiences He allowed me to live through so that now I can share them with you.

I pray that something written on these pages will touch you to act, not necessarily to be a living organ donor (although that would be awesome!), but to intentionally listen to what God is speaking into your life. Read the Bible, pray, seek out other believers, and be the doers of His direction in your life. I have not always done these things, but now that I have, I live life with a different perspective and a renewed sense of energy and purpose.

When thinking about all the parts to this story and all the people involved, directly or indirectly, I'm sure I will leave someone out, but please know I thank each and every one who prayed for me, listened to me question God's intentions, brought me a meal, sent me an encouraging text or email, called me on the phone, and those who continue to walk beside me through this life I'm privileged to live. Oh, and just so you know, I changed some people's names throughout the book to respect their privacy. I tried to ask everyone involved if they would allow me to use their name or another name for them. Some names were not changed just because it either didn't affect the story or they were okay with me using their real names.

Lord and Savior Jesus Christ

First and foremost, I have to thank my Lord and Savior Jesus Christ for allowing me to be a small part of His bigger plan. Thank you, Lord, for plucking me back from the brink of suicide many years ago and taking me on a journey I could never image for myself. Thank you for your wonderful grace that saw me through some of the ugliest times of my life while loving me through it all. Thank you for surrounding me with people who show me how to live a "Godly" life that's not perfect, but one that attempts to shine Your light to others who I come in contact with every day. And, thank you for putting me in a place for me to hear You and for speaking to me in a way that got my attention. I pray every day for Your blessings to be poured out on me and for You to walk with me every step of the way.

My Rock, Tom

The next big thank you goes to my wonderful husband, Tom. You came into my life when I needed you most and you've stuck by me through thick and thin. You never doubted my decision to give a kidney, nor my indecisions when I couldn't figure out what God was directing me to do. Although our relatively short story has suffered some dark times, God always finds a way to bring us back together. I can never repay you nor thank you enough for letting go of your dream to own your own business and move to Troy in order to save our marriage. I am forever grateful for your selflessness and your Godly leadership in our home as well as with others you lead and serve every day.

Mom, Dad, and Courtney

To my mother, father, and sister, I love you more than you know. You've always had my best interest at heart though I haven't always appreciated your concerns. I know I have not always made you proud, and for that I am sorry. I always knew you loved me through all my bad decisions and for that I am eternally thankful. I pray Dad is in heaven smiling and bragging like he always did, letting God see how much he loves us. Maybe he didn't always show us while he was here, but deep down I knew he did.

My Kiddos, Ann-Ashton and Camp

To my children, Ann-Ashton and Camp, I am forever thankful for your love and concern for me over the years. I haven't always been the best mom, and for that I am sorry, but I want you to know I love you to the moon and back! I am so proud of both of you and excited to see what the future holds for you and your future families.

Church Family

To my church, Church of the Highlands, church friends, and Dream Team members who were there in the beginning. Thank you all for being the church where Tom and I landed and the friends we still hold dear. We miss all of you in Birmingham and hope to be back there one day. Everyone who supported Tom and I through the events of 2014 with your words of wisdom, prayers, food, etc. we are forever grateful. I cannot imagine this story without you. Donna started this story with a story of her own. Although we have lost touch, I would love for her to know how much I still admire the grace she displayed when everything seemed ready to take her down. I pray she is still healthy and living a full and rewarding life with her boys.

UAB Transplant Team and Fellow Chain Members

There are truly not enough words to express the admiration and gratitude I have for the UAB kidney transplant teams! They are doing God's work every day and I pray they continue to do what He directs of them for a long time to come. Dr. Locke and all of the other surgeons, the intake nurses (especially UAB Jill!), and all of the people involved in coordinating donors and recipients, they all have the patience of Job and take care of patients and potential patients with love and respect that goes above and beyond anything I've ever seen in the medical field. Fellow chain members, I am honored and humbled to be part of a world-wide phenomenon. Our small links in this chain of miracles is a testament to the grand plan God has for each and every one of us.

I continue to pray for each of the chain members

to live long, healthy, and prosperous lives. To those of you I know and have meet since 2014, I thank God for allowing our paths to cross. For those of you who came after #31 (That's how we acknowledge each other, "Hello, I'm Kelly, #31.") I say, "welcome to the club!" You are a part of something so much bigger than yourselves and a part of an amazing story that continues to grow with each and every one of you.

Mary and Her Family

I am so privileged to know Mary and to be a part of her story. Although this book chronicles my story, she and her family have one just as intriguing. I have an alert on my phone for the 11th of every month to remind me of what happened on December 11, 2014 and although we don't always "talk" on that day, it serves as a reminder that I should never take life or others for granted. Our lives are precious and we are but "a mist that appears for a little time and then vanishes." (James 4:14-NIV)

I pray for Mary's continued good health and strength. I praise her, her family, and God for doing what they did to make sure she got the medical attention she needed when she needed it. I also pray she and I will remain life-long friends and continue to share what God did in both of our lives.

In His Grace,

Kelly, #31

INTRODUCTION

He said to them, "It is not for you to know times or seasons that the Father has fixed by his own authority."

— Acts 1:7 (NIV)

As I approached the greeters at Door 3, Doug met me with a huge smile saying, "I hear you're going to donate a kidney! You're taking this 'servant' thing to a whole new level, aren't you?"

Smiling and agreeing with Doug about my recent approval to become a living organ donor, I was somewhat taken aback by his statement. *Taking this servant thing to a whole new level.* Huh, during the past 9 months I had thought about a lot of things, but I had not thought about what was getting ready to happen quite like Doug. I did realize at that moment, my life as a Christian was forever changed.

That exchange in the halls of our church came after many months of struggling to make the decision to become a living organ donor. I had spoken to countless friends and family for advice. I had consulted numerous physicians and nurses in organ transplant surgery about all the risks. And, I had prayed like I had never prayed before for the Lord to give me peace about the decision, whatever the final decision might be. So, why was I so stunned to hear Doug congratulate me on my latest news?

This book chronicles my life during 2014, examining how I grew as a believer, and how I ultimately decided to become a living organ donor. It's not a story unlike others who are organ donors, but for whatever reason, the Lord decided to really work on me during this time. It is my hope in sharing this journey others will see themselves in some of the places I found myself. I hope readers can relate to my struggles, recognize themselves in my ups and downs, and learn to hear God speaking to them just as He did to me.

The Calm Before the Storm

Have you ever had a slow period in your life? You know, when there's nothing really "big" happening. No births. No weddings. No deaths. No change of jobs. No major life changes, period. Believe it or not, but I had one of those, one time. Notice I said, *one time*. I had not experienced a *slow period* in quite some time, but in the winter of 2013-14, I found myself in such a place.

Let me back up just a bit. This *slow period* was more one of adjusting than of being boring. I had just come out of probably the busiest season of my life prior to this *slow period*. I had finished and successfully defended my dissertation in the spring of 2013, left my job of 17 years, and started a new job at a university two hours away from my home. So, to say my life had *slowed down* was really a misnomer. In a sense, I was starting over. I had taught elementary art for 17 years and now I was teaching freshmen in college, I had lived at my current address for about four years, and I had remarried two years prior, so you could say I was still in an "adjustment" phase.

The fact I was 49 staring down my 50th birthday was also a factor. The older we get, the less likely many of us are willing to accept major change. At least it seemed that way to me, and little did I know I was about to embark on a year of major changes like I had never seen before.

My weeks consisted of driving two hours every Monday morning to my new job in the college town, teaching 4-5 classes through Thursday, and then driving home Thursday evenings. While in the college town, I lived with wonderful friends and colleagues. From Thursday to Sunday, I tried to live my "normal" life back home. You know, doing laundry, cleaning, paying bills, dealing with my teenage daughter's drama, spending quality time with my husband Tom, and leading a greeter team at my church.

Needless to say, this was not a normal work week, but it was my work week for a period of time and I had to make the best of it. It was new and exciting, so, in a way, it was a welcomed change.

Struggles of 2013

While writing this book, I looked in journals I kept at the time and during 2013 life was anything but "smooth." I wrote a lot about struggling with a plethora of issues and surrendering. Surrendering as in COMPLETELY surrendering my life to God. Surrendering not just *parts* of my life, but completely surrendering everything over to Him.

I wrote about fights with my husband, Tom, over money and the lack of time we spent together. We had been financially strapped even before we got married and when I took a job two hours away with a pay cut of $11,000, we were struggling even more. Tom was also trying to get his own construction business off the ground with no working capital, so our personal finances were tapped out.

Because we were struggling financially our personal time together was also suffering. Tom would work extra jobs, usually on the weekends, so what little time we had together on the weekends quickly got eaten up by him working other jobs. When we were together, he was exhausted from all the work he was doing and I always seemed to be playing catch-up. Our time was not spent forging a strong relationship.

I saw us slowly slipping apart and I wasn't sure what to do about it. I felt doomed and believed our marriage was bound to end in divorce unless things took a turn for the better, and fast.

Teaching at the university level had been my dream for many, many years and now I was wondering if earning a Ph.D. and landing a university teaching job was really worth it. I was in deep financial debt after taking out several federal loans to pay for graduate school and to help Tom with some of the financial issues he brought to the marriage. Life was a struggle to say the least.

I also journaled about what I thought our purpose as a couple really was. I felt the Lord was telling me to start a blog with Tom and to write about our story. First of all, this sounds so funny writing about this now. If Tom has to read, much less write, about something, it has to be an article on ESPN.com or a post on Facebook! The thought of writing a blog about "us" was not anywhere on Tom's radar!

Earlier in 2013 I felt the Lord urging me to say something to Tom about it. It was actually during the 2013 Super Bowl game. I waited until half-time and yelled out, "Okay! Fine, I'll say something!" My yelling toward the ceiling got Tom's attention. I told him I felt like God had been urging me to mention the idea of us writing about our story, maybe in a blog.

He laughed!

Tom obviously had not received the same God memo as I had and I felt crazy for even mentioning it. I told him it was fine, but to think about it. I don't think he ever thought of it again, but the thought stayed with me for a long time. We do have an interesting, God-directed story, so I thought maybe that was the blog or book we were supposed to write or maybe God was leading me to write something else....

JANUARY

*"I will instruct you and teach you in the way
you should go; I will counsel you with my
eye upon you."*

— PSALM 32:8 (NIV)

Who Would Be the Next Me?

In the middle of this *slow period*, our church
leaders were asking those of us in leadership
positions to look for the next "us". In other words,
who would replace me once I moved on to another
position? First of all, I had no plans of moving on. I
was perfectly happy co-leading a great group of men
and women every other Sunday as greeters at the

11:30 AM service. But, the question was put before us and I began to ponder it.

As I contemplated who I wanted to talk with about their next position of leadership, I realized I probably would in fact, not stay a leader much longer. I loved leading, but the drive back and forth for my job and trying to lead a normal life just weren't meshing very well. Although I was not ready to step down at the time, I instinctively knew, I would eventually step down. I just had no idea when or where I would go.

Our church, Church of the Highlands, is located in Birmingham, Alabama, and is considered a megachurch. Growing up in a small town with only a handful of churches, this megachurch idea was foreign to me. When Tom and I first started dating, we wanted to go to church together, but we didn't necessarily want to attend a church like what we were accustomed to in our respective hometowns. We were just getting to know each other and our families, so I think we wanted to begin our search for a church with a clean slate. We did a Google search scouting out potential churches. I know, not really spirit-led, was it? No, not at first glance, but the Lord definitely led us there for a reason.

When we joined the church in 2010, I knew I

wanted to be a door greeter. I loved the way those energetic and friendly folks greeted us every Sunday as we entered the church. After going through a divorce a few years back and not feeling welcomed at my former church, I desperately wanted to be accepted in church and I wanted whatever those people had! Tom and I proceeded to go through what is called the Growth Track (four "classes" that help you understand the history and mission of the church, find your purpose, and get you plugged in to serve on the Dream Team).

The Dream Team is what Highlands calls its volunteers. There's a great story about how the volunteers came to be known as the Dream Team, but that's another story for our pastor, Pastor Chris Hodges, to share. Those who greet people entering the church doors, usher folks to a seat, direct cars where to park, man a coffee stand, help in the kids' area, lead a small group, etc. are all part of the Dream Team.

Tom first thought he wanted to serve on the worship team because of his music and missionary background, but after realizing the time commitment necessary for leading worship, he decided to serve as an usher. He served as an usher for a while and eventually moved into a leadership position. I served for a few years as a greeter and then I also started taking on more responsibilities in leadership. Tom and I were both leading our respective teams in January of 2014.

This whole idea of finding the next "us" was not a new idea at our church. The church is big on helping people find their purpose and moving to their next steps in their walk with the Lord, so this was just par for the course with all Dream Team members moving on to leadership positions.

Our greeter team consisted of over 50 people of which 20-30 regularly showed up to greet people at one of the five services the church has each Sunday. My co-leader, Lee and I led the 11:30 AM service every other Sunday. I loved leading this team! On our designated Sunday, my co-leader, Lee, and myself held a quick meeting to inform our team where they would be serving for the day (outside, main doors, sanctuary doors, etc.), led a short devotional, and then always ended in prayer.

So, when Lee and I were tasked to find the next "us", I wrestled with the idea of ever leaving the greeter team. Although I loved serving, I was beginning to feel burned out with new job responsibilities, family, a fairly new marriage, etc., but I didn't share this with Lee. I guess I thought if someone did want to step up, then I would have my "out" once I decided what I wanted to do next. So, in January 2014, I had no intentions of stepping down any time soon. Evidently, God had other plans.

21 Days of Prayer & Fasting

Lee had suggested we pray about finding the next "us" and then each of us would start talking to our potential replacements after we finished our 21 Days of Prayer in January 2014.

Every January our church participates in "21 Days of Prayer and Fasting" and 2014 was no different. Every morning at 6:00 AM for 21 days, Pastor Chris Hodges, or one of the 19 campus pastors, leads a short devotional and worship teams perform a few worship songs. Then there is about 30 minutes for private, individual prayer, and the service ends with 15 minutes of corporate prayer. Many of the 19 campuses have live, face-to-face worship services, while the prayer service is streamed from the main campus in Birmingham. If we're unable to go to a church for the service, then we have the option to watch the service online.

Instead of attending a live service I would watch the service online while getting ready for work.

Many times, Tom and I would call or Skype during the service and pray together. I journaled about the topic of the short devotional and made notes about our prayers that we shared each day.

Tom and I prayed those 21 days for each other, our financial situation, our families, our jobs, and for others.

Journal Entry

January 17, 2014: The word "rest" has popped up in all of my readings this week. Huh....maybe I need to rest knowing the Lord has this!

FEBRUARY

If anyone has material possessions and sees a
brother or sister in need but has no pity
on them, how can the love of God be in
that person?

— 1 John 3:17 (NIV)

Divide and Conquer

At the end of 21 Days of Prayer, Lee and I decided it was best to divide and conquer the challenge of finding the next "us." On one particular Sunday, we agreed who each of us would talk to and then report back to the other at the end of the service.

I spoke to a few of our greeters before the service started and several of them shared their interest in possibly moving into a different position or one of leadership. Several said they would pray about what might be their next steps and would get back to me soon. Easy, peasy....until I got to Donna.

Donna was a woman who was about my age, a single mom of two boys, who worked full-time, and who served as a dependable greeter every month. She was very personable and always reliable, so I decided I would talk to her about what she thought her next step might be as a greeter. Secretly I had already put her on my list of future door captains, thinking that would be a perfect place for her to move into as her next area of leadership.

Because our team was so large, greeters were broken down into greeters, door captains, and then team leaders. This hierarchy allowed Lee and me to focus on the "big picture" operations of running a team of greeters during the church service. Door captains were responsible for not only keeping doorways flowing freely, but for personally knowing the greeters assigned to their particular door and offering them prayer in the weeks between services. Donna had been a greeter for quite some time, so moving into a door captain position was her obvious next move.

I distinctly remember talking to Donna in the area we call Dream Team Central (DTC). DTC is an area where all Dream Teamers – ushers, greeters, worship team members, etc. – meet to check in, grab a donut and a cup of coffee, get their assignments for the day, and pray before going to their assigned place for the next service. The 11:30 AM service was already in progress, but those of us who had finished serving were hanging out in DTC chatting and grabbing our winter coats and handbags before we headed to our cars.

Before I left, I saw Donna sitting in DTC. We exchanged niceties for a few minutes and I noticed she looked really tired, but I didn't think much about it. I begin to talk to her about greeting and then asked if she had ever thought about moving into a leadership role with the greeter team and she said she had. I thought, "Oh, good, this is going to be an easy one!" She then told me she was flattered I would ask her, but she would have to decline. My spirits went from soaring to taking a downward dive! I thought, well, shoot, I would have to erase her from my list of possible door captains already stirring around in my head! But, I told her it was fine. If she wanted to think on it or pray about it, I understood. She didn't need to think about it. She knew she couldn't.

She very bluntly told me she was about to begin dialysis and she needed us to pray for her. Whoa, wait, what? What did she just say? Dialysis? Prayers? Hold on, what did she just say?!?!?

I was dumbfounded! How did we as a greeter group not know this? It was our jobs as leaders to know the needs of our teams and to pray for them. How did I not know?

I did know Donna had Lupus, but I didn't know just how sick she really was or what was even involved with someone who has the disease. I told her of course we would pray for her, but then asked what else she needed? She said, "Just pray someone has a kidney that matches mine. I'll need a kidney transplant eventually."

In shock, I somehow finished the conversation, found Lee, and shared the news with her. She did not know about Donna's situation either, so it came as a shock to both of us. Our Dream Team leader, Nicole, did know, but told us she didn't know much more other than Donna would begin dialysis very soon.

Snarky Response

Tom and I had been praying together during 21 Days of Prayer and we continued beyond the 21 days. On February 6th (just four days after Donna's announcement) I was praying by myself late one night. I couldn't sleep, so I was lying there just thinking about life in general. I started thinking about Donna and immediately started praying that someone would come forward to donate a kidney and they would be a match for her.

Just as I began to pray for God to find a match for Donna, I heard the Lord say, "Well, you have two."

I literally looked around the room! I didn't hear an audible voice, but I heard the message loud and clear! No one in the house at the time was awake, so I knew it wasn't my housemates, but I looked around anyway. I have to say the voice was a bit snarky. Kind of like, "Well, I could answer your prayer, but so could you."

He was right! I had two, or at least I thought I had two. I have since learned that some people, including my late uncle, are born with only one kidney. But, I was going on the assumption I had two.

All of a sudden, my prayer time stopped and I grabbed my computer to begin Googling "kidney donation." Gotta love some Google! I began seeing all sorts of hospitals and kidney donation groups with information about donation. There are a lot of resources out there! A lot!

I also decided, although it was late, to text our Dream Team leader, Nicole, and ask if she knew what the steps were for becoming a donor. She works for an OB/GYN as a Registered Ultrasound Technologist, and she knew a little about Donna's situation, so I thought why not ask someone in "medicine". That sounds so crazy to say it now! Just because she works for a doctor, I assumed she would "know something." Surprisingly, she did!

Via text, I asked Nicole, "So what would someone have to do if they were thinking about becoming an organ donor?" To my surprise, she was still awake and responded with a few short answers like, blood work, EKG, psychological testing, etc. I think I asked a few more questions, and then she asked me one, "So why do you want to know all this?"

Should I tell her I think God just spoke to me? Should I tell her He was a bit snarky reminding me that I, in fact, have two kidneys? I was not ready to tell anyone just yet, so I kept it to myself and said I was "curious." That seemed to satisfy her for the moment, but I knew she would want to know what led me to start asking questions.

Nicole did give me one piece of information that would lead me toward finding out the real nitty gritty about being tested as an organ donor. She knew the hospital in another state that Donna had been in contact with about her situation. I searched their website, Transplant Living's website, Johns Hopkins Medicine site, and just about ALL of the websites Google pulled up that night. I decided to start looking at those sites the next day.

As I lay there thinking, "Did what I think just happened, really happen? Did God just speak to me?" My mind started to race about what might be involved in order to donate a kidney. I wanted to find out all I could about living organ donation as soon as possible. This feeling of hearing from God had only happened one time before, so I knew it was the Holy Spirit trying to get my attention.

Being Filled with the Holy Spirit

Three years prior to all this happening, my home state of Alabama had been involved with several

severe tornado outbreaks. I was watching the
television coverage one Sunday before getting ready
to go to church and all of a sudden, I got this
overwhelming feeling to do something to help the
victims of the tornados. I could have given blood,
donated clothing and food, or even helped with
clean up, and I did do some of these things, but the
Holy Spirit put another idea on my heart.

As I began to think about what more I could do,
the answer came almost immediately. *Help the
children displaced by the tornados with art projects.*
Bam!

Many children and their families lost everything.
After assisting refugees from Hurricane Katrina a
few years before, I knew art was sometimes the best
way for children to express themselves and to
occupy their time while their parents took care of
finding clothes, food, and shelter at rescue centers.

This idea needed a lot of manpower and
supplies and those needs were found almost
immediately. I needed a name for the group, and
bam, another inspiration came to me. The group
would be called, *Healing Hearts with Art.* Perfect!

To make this long story a little shorter, *Healing
Hearts with Art* received money, supplies, and
manpower far and above what I ever expected. We

went to some of the hardest hit areas and provided a small reprieve through the creation of art to children around the state. We had enough art supplies to continue working with a local school's after-school program for another year after the tornados. Just when we thought we were "finished" at that school, we had enough supplies to donate to another school system where the art teacher lost everything in another series of tornadoes the following year.

Since the events of 2011, I've realized when the Holy Spirit is speaking to me, two things often happen. An idea gets "in" me and I cannot let go until I 1) do something about it, or 2) have an answer. So, I set out to find answers about living organ donation.

I was excited because I knew if this truly was the Holy Spirit, then something big was about to happen! I not only listened and set out to find answers on how to be a donor, but my prayer life dramatically changed that night. I began to pray for direction and purpose and I stopped doing all the talking and listened for God's voice.

Telling Family, Friends, and Donna

I'm still not sure how I finally fell asleep that
particular night in February, but as I woke the next
morning, I still had the feeling of wanting to do
something for Donna.

I told Tom what I was thinking and he was
behind me 100%, but he was about the only one
supporting me.

As I began to tell my family, they all tried to talk
me out of it. I distinctly remember telling my mom
and her response, "What if I need a kidney? What if
your children need one? What if you need one?" I
had to laugh a little. Mom was turning 74 that year
and I told her I thought if she was going to need one,
we would already know! As for my kids, they were,
for the most part, healthy and if they should ever
need a kidney hopefully God would find them one
just like He was finding one for my friend right now.

And as for me, well, I was about to be 50 years
old, so I really didn't foresee any major health
problems where I would need a kidney any time in
the near future.

I felt confident if anyone in my family needed a
kidney, God would provide one. Those fears my
mother mentioned never really entered my mind.

For me a sense of calm and purpose had already settled in.

My sister is a pharmacist and my sister-in-law is a nurse, so they tried to explain the medical implications of giving a kidney and tried to steer me away from beginning the testing and donation process. My daughter, Ann-Ashton, cried thinking I would die. No, "what might happen?" No, "Oh, you're awesome to want to do this for someone!" No, she went straight to the worst possible scenario! My ex-husband wasn't much better, simply asking if my life insurance policy was paid and up-to-date. I knew he was joking, but their concerns did not go unnoticed.

Everyone had my best interest, mainly my life, at heart when they shared their concerns with me, but I was never scared. I never feared anything would go wrong. If God was directing me to do this, He would take care of me. Easy peasy! Well, turns out it was not so easy.

Looking back, I realize the Enemy, the Devil himself, was in my year of decisions as much as the Holy Spirit. The negative reaction from family and friends, although brief and small, could have been enough to stop me, but for whatever reason, I kept going forward. I "heard" them and their concerns, but from the very beginning I had a peace about the decision to at least be tested. The decision to keep continue with the testing process was a whole different matter.

I'm a teacher and researcher, so I needed to have all the facts before I began to seriously consider donating a kidney to anyone. I Googled living transplant donation which led to a plethora of websites that basically all said the same thing (i.e. there were a battery of tests I would need to go through in order to find out if I was healthy enough to donate and to see if I was a match).

Finally, it was time to tell Donna. I honestly can't remember if I called, texted, or saw her at church, but I remember after telling her I wanted to be tested as a possible donor for her that she gave me the contact information for the University of Alabama at Birmingham (UAB) hospital where she was being evaluated. She was shocked and happy to hear a friend was willing to go through the testing process.

She informed me of a hospital she had originally talked to in another state, but because she was a single mom and did not have any family members who lived close, the hospital was afraid she did not have a strong support system to transport her back and forth for treatments. At first I thought how rude to turn someone away, but then I realized they were probably thinking of her situation from a logistics perspective, not in a humanitarian way. Little did they know she had a faith family that would have driven her anywhere if it meant she would get a new kidney and be healed.

No Reason Not To

As I slowly began to talk about the testing process for becoming an organ donor, people started to ask me why I wanted to do this. My first response was always, "Well, I have a friend who needs a kidney and if I don't, who will?" The more I thought about people's reaction to me when I would say, "I want to be tested", my reaction began to change. I started saying, "I can't think of a reason not to."

I honestly could not think of a reason not to at least be tested for the donation. A lot of people asked why I was considering giving a kidney to someone I only *sort of* knew. Donna wasn't family. She wasn't a really close friend, so, why would I?

I tried to think about the whole situation in reverse. What if this were me or one of my family members who needed an organ in order to live?

What if none of my family members were a match, then what? What if I were dependent on a stranger to save my life and live healthy again? Who would step up and save me?

That reflection solidified my decision. I could not find a reason not to at least try. I might not be a match for Donna, but if I didn't go through with the testing I would never know. I also knew if I didn't have the testing done, I would regret not doing it if something ultimately happened to Donna.

While thinking about the many reasons to be tested another memory came back to me. My former brother-in-law had a liver transplant several years prior. He and his twin brother had some autoimmune diseases that attack different parts of the body. My brother-in-law's illness was Primary Sclerosing Cholangitis which destroyed his liver. I remember a time when both brothers spent a lot of time in hospitals and were extremely sick. My brother-in-law was the lucky one. He was able to have stents put in to open his bile ducts, which was a temporary fix until he got so sick that he was put on a liver transplant list for three weeks. Evidently you have to be pretty close to death to even be considered for this type of transplant. A match was found for him in time, but unfortunately, his liver came at the expense of another young man's death. Thankfully, the young man was an organ donor and was a match to my brother-in-law.

My brother-in-law went on to get better and has lived a happy, healthy, and full life for 12 years now. But, the flip side to his story is that his brother was not so lucky. His disease, Pulmonary Fibrosis, attacked his lungs and tragically, he didn't live long enough to receive a lung transplant. I remember thinking, "I wish we could donate body parts when we're living. Why do so many people have to die when there are plenty of living people available to donate or at least be on the organ donor registry?"

Those experiences with transplants where one was saved and one was not, affected me more than I realized. Remembering the time my brother-in-law and his brother needed organ transplants were part of the reason I continued to tell people I couldn't think of a good enough reason not to at least try to be an organ donor for my friend.

My mind was made up; I was going to proceed with the testing process and see where it led me.

Is There Something Wrong with Me?

I initially contacted the first hospital Donna had connected with and they were actually helpful in sharing their requirements for possible living donors. They required a recent pap smear test, abdominal sonogram, EKG test, a lot of blood work, and possibly a colonoscopy. Ugh! Really? A colonoscopy? Okay, fine.

Before the "official" testing began, I decided to go ahead and have the colonoscopy done. For about two years I had suffered with severe stomach pains and digestive issues. I hadn't had a colonoscopy in several years, so I hoped to find out what my stomach issues were all about.

My father always had stomach issues and dealt with ulcers for a long time. I had convinced myself that I too had stomach ulcers, or worse. My son had been diagnosed with Crohn's disease a few years prior, so I thought maybe that was what was wrong with me. I had basically talked myself into being the sick one.

I know you probably don't want to hear about my digestive issues, but here again, the Enemy tried to keep me from going forward in the process. Even as I began to think about all of the requirements needed to become an organ donor I used the excuse of not having the time to go to the doctor almost stop me. I would think, "Well, I really don't have time to take off for any testing, so I'm not even going to bother trying." Really? No Devil, you're not going to stop me from at least trying!

I tried talking myself out of making the appointment numerous times, yet I was willing to live with bottles of Pepto Bismol hidden in every crevice of my life: handbag, bathroom, desk at work, and even in the car. I felt like an alcoholic sneaking a swig of whiskey when I took a gulp of Pepto. I was in horrible pain, but I didn't want anyone else to really know how bad it was. Crazy I know!

I found a gastrointestinal doctor in Birmingham and finally made an appointment. He quizzed me about my symptoms, heard about my family history, and then I told him I was trying to become a living organ donor. All of a sudden the conversation got a little more energetic. He said, "Oh, so you have a lot of reasons to want to know what's going on!" Yes, yes I did. He was impressed and intrigued that I would do such a thing for a friend and realized he needed to find out what was going on with me before I could be considered a donor.

Because I worked most of the week in another

town, I had to schedule the colonoscopy for a time when I knew I had a few days to prep and then rest. If you've never had one of these procedures, let me just say, it is NO fun. The procedure is not what's bad, because you're put under with general anesthesia, but rather the "cleansing" that comes before. You spend the day prior to the procedure getting your digestive tract cleaned out by taking laxatives and drinking some funky orange stuff that after about the third glass starts tasting horrible. Not a fun day. Then they knock you out to do the procedure, so you lose another day to good sleeping meds. Lastly, depending on how you take to anesthesia, you could be fine the next day or a little groggy. So, I knew I would need at least 2-3 days to get through the entire procedure.

Journal Entry

February 06, 2014: I'm feeling convicted about donating a kidney to Donna.
February 09, 2014: Heard from Donna thanking me for offering to be tested!

MARCH

*"Or do you not know that your body is a
temple of the Holy Spirit within you,
whom you have from God? You are not
your own, for you were bought with a
price. So glorify God in your body."*

— 1 CORINTHIANS 6:19-20 (ESV)

A Life with Pepto

I decided to put the colonoscopy procedure off a
few weeks until my university's spring break.
Fun way to spend your spring break, huh? Actually,
not too bad because I scheduled it during the first

weekend of the break, so I was back to normal by Monday.

For a couple of weeks, I worried what the test would reveal. I had already convinced myself there was something terribly wrong with me, but I just needed the doctor to confirm my fears. The call finally came as I was sitting in my office one afternoon.

I was a little taken aback when I recognized it was THE doctor on the other end of the phone. Normally I thought a nurse would make the call with test results or ask you to come back in, not the actual doctor! My first thoughts were, "Oh, no! This must be REALLY bad if HE's calling me!"

The doctor began by saying things looked good and he saw no major issues. I was dumbfounded. You mean there is nothing really wrong with me? Then why do I feel so badly and why are you calling me? He continued with, "Oh, I do think you have Irritable Bowel Syndrome (IBS), but that's treatable." Seriously? That was it, IBS?

I was relieved and sort of stumped at the same time. The pain had been so severe; I was really expecting him to say something more serious than IBS. Remember, I had literally lived with a bottle of Pepto-Bismol attached to me for two years. I thanked him and set up another appointment to determine my treatment and to obtain my records for UAB Hospital. He put me on some meds for a few months to help with the pain and to start correcting some of the issues. He also told me to avoid or lessen some foods like carbonated drinks, and other things that might be upsetting my stomach and he would see me in another month or so.

Surprisingly, between those two visits, I started eliminating foods I thought might be causing my problems. By the time I returned to his office I had determined that chocolate, milk, and Diet Mountain Dews were my biggest culprits. He was impressed I had taken the time to figure out what foods were bothering me. Me, not so much. I told him, "If you had put me on a deserted island and said, 'Okay, you can take three foods with you,' guess which ones would have been at the top of my list? You guessed it: chocolate, milk, and Diet Mountain Dews!" This was a huge blow to my menu selections!

So, I didn't have ulcers AND my favorite foods were the reason I felt terrible. Great! Of course, everyone was happy for me to find out I wasn't really sick, but I was frustrated. Even thinking about it now, I'm not really sure why. Did I want to be sick?

No, I don't think so. That would be weird. Who wishes themselves sick?

I now believe it was the Enemy once again trying to knock me down. I had taken over a month to have the test done and another few weeks to determine what were my triggers. Doubt was creeping in and I began to think I might never be approved as a living organ donor.

Learning to Wait

Like most of us, I wanted all of these tests, their results, and my approval to be an organ donor to happen in the blink of an eye. But, like most things in life, it wasn't happening according to my schedule.

I believed God wanted me to do this, so why was it taking so long? I knew they could not confirm me as an organ donor with only one test, but I was hoping the process would move along a little faster. Again, this was the Enemy's way of trying to stop the process altogether and he almost succeeded.

If it weren't for Donna being so sick and still in need of a kidney, I might have given up. Because I knew she was still sick and the hospital had yet to find a match for her, I knew I couldn't stop yet.

I wanted to move along with the living donor tests at UAB, but they needed the most current physical exam, pap smear, and mammogram from my gynecologist and I had not been to the doctor in almost a year. So, you guessed it, I had to have all of that done before UAB would even talk to me.

Because I was still living and working two hours from my home and from where my doctor was located, finding time to schedule the visit seemed futile until I finished the school semester. So, again, I waited.

But, I decided there was something I could do while I waited; I could pray. I could pray and I could ask others to pray, and pray they did. My husband, Tom, and I shared with our families, our respective small groups, the teams we led at church, and the church in general through weekly prayer requests what I had decided to do and asked if they would join us in prayer. We asked for prayers that all of my tests would come back clear and that I would move along in the process without any problems. We asked for prayers for Donna, as well as for God to find her a kidney match soon.

The support from everyone was amazing! Everyone agreed to pray hard and immediately. We felt the love and support from those prayers and it

kept me focused on the purpose, not on the wait.
The wait was still hard, but knowing so many people
were praying for me made it a bit more bearable.

Tat Pact

In late March, several gals who were in graduate
school with me attended The International
Congress of Qualitative Inquiry conference in
Illinois. Three of us made a pact a few years back
that when we finished our Ph.D. degrees, we would
all get tattoos. Many people who begin a Ph.D. do
not finish and we were determined not to be another
statistic. So, what better way to assure we would
finish than to promise to get tats together?

The reason we decided on tattoos as a way to
celebrate our accomplishments, I do not know.
When the pact was first made, we said we would get
"Ph.D." tattooed somewhere on our bodies. Two of
us did not have any tattoos, so we were trying to
think of a small, insignificant place to put one. I
thought maybe behind my ear, shoulder, etc. I really
had no idea where I would put a tat.

The pact was all but forgotten until we were
driving to the conference in 2014. The three of us
reminisced about the last time we were at the

conference working on our degrees, made the pact to finish, and get tattoos. All three of us finished and obtained a teaching position in three different universities, but this was the first time we had been together since the tat pact was made. It was time to make good on our bet.

Since we had a few years to think about getting a tat, none of us now wanted "Ph.D." tattooed on our bodies. We had accomplished a feat many do not ever attain, so we wanted a tat with a more personal meaning to each of us.

Tammi, the gal who already had two tats, decided she wanted the Tree of Life on her back with several different colors. Jackie, the other gal who did not have a tat, wanted a quote that meant a lot to her on her shoulder. I decided I wanted a quote by Michelangelo, "Ancora Imparo" tattooed on my wrist. This quote means "I am still learning." Michelangelo said this when he was in his eighties and I thought if someone as accomplished as he could make a statement like that late in his life, then I, too, wanted that to be my life's mantra even though I was only 49 at the time.

Somehow I drew the short straw and was the first one of the three to get her tat. We found a super clean tattoo shop with some great artists willing to pacify three "older" women wanting tats.

I decided I was okay with having my tat show on my wrist, so I selected the font and double-checked the Italian spelling and we were good to go. Jackie went with me to see the process and to hold my hand if necessary.

My tattoo artist and I chit-chatted for a few minutes and when he found out I was an art teacher he shared his portfolio with me. I was impressed and felt even better about his abilities to do a good job with my tat. I was not, however, ready for the pain.

I'm not sure what I was expecting. I thought maybe he would give me a heads-up when he was about to start or maybe he would give me a sampling of how it would feel. Nope! None of that! He went straight in!

As soon as he started, my body tensed and although I didn't scream, I wanted to. I couldn't believe it! It was excruciating! I stopped talking mid-sentence and looked at Jackie with what must have startled her as much as the pain was hurting me. She immediately started talking as fast as she could to me in order to distract me from the pain. I have no idea what she said, but I remember her telling me random stuff just to keep me from screaming out in pain.

And, just like that, it was over.

It was sort of like what many say about giving birth, you eventually forget the pain and you'll do it again. Pretty much what I felt and said shortly after it was finished. I was extremely happy with how it turned out. I haven't gotten another tat yet, but I really want one.

I had not talked about it much to Tom or my family because I didn't think I had to. They all knew I wanted one, but didn't say much about it. My mom did try to talk me out of it, but I just thought she didn't want me doing something she thought I might regret later.

Believe it or not, but that tattoo has been a wonderful talking point for me with students, friends, and complete strangers. People ask me what it says, what it means, etc. I even do a show-and-tell when I'm beginning a new class each semester. I tell my new students if Michelangelo could say he was still learning in his late eighties, then surely, I can learn something new in my fifties (I usually mumble that last part!). Part of me hopes they will think I'm the "cool" teacher, but more importantly I hope they will recognize the essence of what it truly means—that we never stop learning.

Journal Entry

*March 27, 2014: (Tom's Prayer) Give Kelly peace
today to get things done today and ready for her trip.
Keep her mind open to recognize the devil and to
rebuke him. Help us both to be Heavenly-minded and
know that You are in control!*

APRIL

"The Lord is not slow to fulfill his promise as some count slowness, but is patient toward you, not wishing that any should perish, but that all should reach repentance."

— 2 Peter 3:9 (NIV)

The Waiting Game

As some of my preliminary health tests began to be checked off my list, the semester at the university also came to a close. Although the time between spring break and the end of the semester was only about two months, it felt like eternity.

As I looked through my journals from 2014 I realized not much happened during the month of April. Like N-O-T-H-I-N-G! There were no more tests until May. There were no major events. There were no developments with finding Donna a match for a new kidney. So, what was I to do?

This "in-between" time is often the hardest time for believers. We "think" God has spoken to us and is directing us to do something in His name and then nothing. No more words of wisdom. No more snarky voices. Nothing.

To be perfectly honest, I began to doubt I was doing the right thing. Maybe I really didn't hear God's voice. Maybe it was just me wanting to help my friend, especially when her life was in danger. Maybe it just wasn't meant to be. Maybe, maybe, maybe!

That was the Enemy talking! He was sneaking into my head, again.

So, what can we do when we're waiting?

As I began debating God (like we can "debate" Him!) about what I was supposed to do, I still didn't hear a response. Life went on. I survived my second semester teaching at the university and I was settling into a life spent living in two places. Life was moving along pretty well.

Tom and I continued to pray for my tests to happen sooner rather than later, for Donna's health, and for direction in what, exactly, I was supposed to do.

Continuing to pray the same prayers doesn't mean God is really busy and one day He *finally* gets to us, like a patient waiting to see the doctor. He hears our prayers the first time and every time afterwards. It does mean WE should be persistent in SEEKING Him. We are not giving up until we hear from Him!

While writing a recent blog post about "waiting" I was reminded of the scripture in 1 Peter, *"Humble yourselves, therefore under God's mighty hand and he will exalt you in due time. Cast all your anxiety on him because he cares for you"* (1 Peter 5:6-7- NIV).

As we consistently pray for things in our lives, we also need to humble ourselves before Him and *submit to His ways*, He will exalt us in due time.

I researched "due time" and found one definition that said, "eventually at an appropriate time." That phrase, "at an appropriate time," really struck me as interesting especially now that I know the end of this story. At an appropriate time, may not be OUR time, but in HIS time because He knows when that is! We *think* we do, but most likely we do not.

So, even though not much happened in the way of testing or major events with Donna or me during April, *something* was happening, but I just couldn't see it. He heard my prayers and He was working things out for everyone's good and in His due time.

Learning from Other Times of Waiting

I've been in situations where I didn't think I was hearing from God, so I needed to remember those situations and what I did while I was waiting.

One thing I remembered doing was checking my heart. I would ask myself several questions:

- Where am I with Him *right now?*
- Have I been *steadfast* in my prayer life?
- Have I truly been *purposeful* in my prayers?
- Have I *stopped and listened* for His response during my prayer time?

Many times, I was "consistent" with my prayer life, but not "purposeful". How can one be consistent, but not purposeful? Easy. We can get in a rut and just pray the same prayers we always pray just to say we've prayed or just hoping He will hear us and finally answer them.

We can't always see this until we're on the other side of an event. We may pray the same prayers over and over without really thinking about the words we are using and therefore the words become rote and meaningless. Not that they aren't sincere, but they just begin to not mean much if we're saying the same thing, the same way with every prayer.

Another idea I remembered during this time of waiting was to objectively look at my struggles. I would ask myself questions like:

- *When and how* have I struggled to find solutions to issues in the past?
- What happened in the *middle* of those struggles?
- What happened *at the end* of those struggles?
- *What did I learn* from those experiences?

Past and present struggles tend to get me down, at least for a little while. In the middle of a struggle I often think there is no way out, but I've learned to seek the Lord's will. If He's going to supernaturally "fix" the issue, great! But if He's teaching me something, I need to take note and realize what "it" is. What does He want me to learn as I'm in the middle of this struggle?

Lastly, I need to learn from the struggles I've been through. This is similar to analyzing my struggles, but I have to look at times when I learned something brand new, not just when I am struggling with something I already know. Some of the questions I would ask myself were:

- *When* did I learn something new?
- *Why* did I learn it? (Work requirement or personal growth?)
- *Who* taught me this new thing? (The Lord himself or did He connect me with others who knew how to teach me?)
- Once I learned this new lesson, *how* did it help me in my life?
- *What* can I do now that I've learned this new thing?

Recently, some "new" adventures have come my way. I began leading one of our church's small groups in person and online and taking over the art education responsibilities from a colleague who is preparing to retire. Although I've done other small groups, I've never done one both face-to-face AND online. And, I've been teaching art for over 20 years, but teaching these particular art education classes and being responsible for art education majors is all new for me.

Dark Night Psalms

While writing this book, I ran across one of my old blog posts about the Dark Night Psalms. I had never heard of these Psalms before I wrote that particular post (Ah-ha! A new lesson!), so I was interested in what these Psalms were all about. These particular Psalms are called the Dark Night of the Soul or the Dark Night Psalms. Evidently Psalms 13, 42, 46, 59, 77, 88, 92, and 143 are specifically considered the Dark Night ones. It's basically a time when you don't think you're hearing from the Lord.

Although I ultimately did hear from the Lord during those dark nights in April and May 2014, the Dark Night Psalms serve as a great reminder for the next time I don't think I'm hearing God's voice. The Soul Shepherding website describes these times as feeling "spiritually dry and distant from God". The author also describes it as a time of "trial" where

God is working to deepen our journey of dependence on Him.

When I read that last sentence I had a light bulb moment! That's EXACTLY what God was doing in me during 2014! I needed to dig in and not just go through the motions. I should look at my past struggles and examine what I learned from surviving all of them. It is also essential to search through lessons He leads me through in the moment they are happening and understand what He's trying to teach me.

Journal Entry

April 29, 2014:
Today was the day after a huge tornado outbreak crossed through Mississippi, Alabama, and Tennessee. The is becoming an "expected" event every year about this time! Please protect all of those affected by the tornados and keep us all safe.

MAY

*"More than that, we rejoice in our sufferings,
knowing that suffering produces
endurance, and endurance produces
character, and character produces hope."*

— ROMANS 5:3-4 (ESV)

Let the Testing Begin

While nothing really happened in the way of tests or advancement in the donation process during April, May, was a whole different story. Once university finals were over and grades were successfully submitted I had a few weeks before I had to be back to Troy to teach the summer sessions, so I decided to get as many of the tests done as I could.

People have asked how Tom and I paid for all these tests, especially with all of our financial issues. Luckily when you're the one trying to donate, the recipient's insurance picks up most of the expenses. Tests like the colonoscopy and the annual pap smear and mammogram were tests I paid for because they were part of my regular preventive regimen. The colonoscopy was not covered by Donna's insurance because UAB didn't require that test, but I felt compelled to have it done due to the pain I had experienced for the past two years.

The biggest group of tests took place all in one day at UAB Hospital. I had to catch urine for a day or so before going to the hospital and then parade a very full gallon milk jug in a brown grocery bag to the hospital for testing. Lovely!

After I arrived at the hospital in the area where I thought I was supposed to be, I was instructed to go to a different building all while lugging my brown grocery bag. Thankfully I had taken a jacket with me because after all the walking from the parking deck and across the hospital, I began to "leak." Well, not me, but rather my pitcher of pee. Embarrassing! So, when I was finally able to find an empty seat in the huge waiting room, I covered the bag with my jacket. There were a lot of people who didn't seem to notice I was even there, nor did they care what I was doing, so hopefully no one noticed.

Thinking I was safely seated and had hidden my embarrassing pitcher of leaking pee, I forgot I would eventually have to get up when my name was called. Being by myself made what felt like a huge spotlight on me even bigger. The people in that waiting room were visibly sick and probably didn't care who I was or why I was there. I just wanted to slink under the seat or secretly slip out the door somehow, but there seemed to be no escape route visible. I would have to wait it out and carry my pee jug with as much dignity as I could muster.

By the time my name was called, many of the people had left the waiting area or had been called back for their own testing appointments. I'm not sure if I felt more or less in the spotlight by then, but I know I was still worried about how I would get my jug into the exam room without the bag tearing or leaking even more. I decided I would scoop it up with my jacket and pray no one saw my leaking tinkle vessel. Problem solved!

Finally, my name was called! As I entered the door where I was being summoned, a jovial male nurse greeted me. While he butchered my last name, as most people do, he proceeded to direct me to the back offices while asking to take my urine sample from me. Oh, no, horror moment again! Now, how to do the handoff without getting him and me wet while saving face all at the same time. Somehow I apologized for the "leaking" and he seemed undeterred by my lack of stabilization skills.

He set aside the paper sack and led me back to an area for drawing blood. He kept me distracted by talking to me the entire time he stuck me and drew about TWENTY vials of blood. Seriously, he did! When I looked over at his pile of vials I wondered if I would have enough blood still in me to walk out of the hospital.

He was curious about what tests I was having done. I was about the only "healthy" person in the waiting area so, he was probably a bit perplexed about why I was there. I don't mean to boast about being the only healthy person in the hospital (I'm sure there were others), but more than once I noticed hospital personnel were not accustomed to seeing healthy people coming in for these types of tests. Being a relatively healthy person coming in for a battery of tests evidently throws up red flags and stirs curiosities. I gave him the short version of my story and he told me it was a great thing for me to do and wished me well.

After the bloodletting phase of my test day, I was led from station to station for different evaluations. There was an EKG stop, a mental health evaluation, and an abdominal sonogram. It was an all-day affair!

To my surprise, I was told I had high cholesterol and there was a cyst on one of my kidneys. The doctors assured me the cyst was probably nothing. They said a lot of people have cysts on their kidneys and never have any problems. I was a little shocked, but decided not to worry too much about the cyst, at least for now.

Testing: Round 2

In late May, I was able to get an appointment with my gynecologist for all of those other "fun" tests. Not at all "fun," but necessary nonetheless. Those tests consisted of an annual pap smear, mammogram, and blood work. Yes, more blood work!

When I told the doctor, I would need a copy of my exam sent to UAB, he too became a bit curious. We actually attend the same church and knew each other through Nicole, my friend and Dream Team leader who works as an ultrasound technician for the doctor. Knowing me a bit more than just a patient, he was naturally curious about the process I was going through to become a living organ donor. Once again, I briefly told him my story and what had happened since January, minus the part about God speaking to me, and he praised me for wanting go through the testing process.

After sharing my story numerous times, I had it down to a great elevator speech. I was still not comfortable telling people, even believers, that I believed God had spoken to me and led me down this path. But why was I afraid to share this part of the story? Would people think I was crazy? Would they think I was making it up? Would this information change the way they treated me? Was I just fearful of being judged?

It was probably all of those things and more. Even though I felt confident God had in deed spoken to me that night in February and I was continuing to do what I thought He wanted me to do, I still had my doubts of what *others* would think of me if I shared this part of the story.

May Coming to a Close

As May came to a close I was relieved that all of the tests were behind me, but I was still anxious about when I would find out if I was a match or not. Luckily, summer classes were starting back, so my attention was diverted, at least for a few weeks.

Knowing I had stepped out in faith to do what I believed God wanted me to do was a weight off my shoulders, but I really didn't know where the next phase of this adventure would take me. Thinking back about it now, I guess I really had not thought much past getting the testing done. I had several surgeries before, so the surgery part of possibly being a match for a friend didn't bother me at all. I really never thought about the severity of the surgery even though it would be the biggest part of my journey.

Journal Entry

May 02, 2014:
Prayers for Donna. Praying you find a donor for her quickly and if is to be me, then please make that clear. Allow Tom and I to find others to pray for and with.

JUNE

"The heart of man plans his way, but
the LORD establishes his steps."

— PROVERBS 16:9 (ESV)

THE Call

In the early part of June, I was shopping in the local Michael's store when I received a phone call. When I looked at the caller ID I saw it was "UAB Jill," the case coordinator and nurse for potential kidney donors. Immediately I realized this was THE Call. It was the call that could possibly tell me I was, or was not, a match to Donna. Within seconds I made a decision to answer the call in the

middle of the store. I hate when people walk around
a store or stand in a checkout line talking on their
phones, but I felt like I had to answer this call.

As I answered, UAB Jill asked if I could talk and
without thinking, I softly said, "Yes." She told me she
had some news and a question. Again, I said okay, as
I anticipated her "news" to be that I was a match
for Donna.

I can't remember exactly how she told me, but
her news was that I was NOT a match to Donna. I
was dumbfounded. My knees buckled and I wanted
to cry. Being in the middle of a busy craft store, I
knew I couldn't drop to my knees and scream like I
wanted to, so I hung on, but I barely remember what
she said next.

After telling me how sorry she was that I wasn't
a match for Donna, she needed to ask me a question.
I again said, "okay," while still trying to keep my
composure, and then she asked if I wanted to go
ahead in the donation process. I honestly don't
remember if I asked her what that meant or not, but
I'm pretty sure I didn't know what she meant.

I vaguely remember her explaining to me that if I
went ahead in the process, it might mean Donna
could receive a kidney sooner. Later I learned UAB
has a compatibility program, as do many kidney

donation hospitals, that when a person agrees to donate a kidney on behalf of their friend or family member, they agree to donate to a stranger. Then that person's friend or family member could get a kidney faster. Basically, it's a numbers game. By having more people in the pool of donors, it makes sense that recipients would have a better chance to get a donor kidney sooner than with the normal get-on-a-list-and-wait process.

I honestly don't remember any more of the conversation. I was so upset, I told UAB Jill that I would need to think about it, talk to my family, and get back to her. I do remember her telling me to take my time and she would be in touch.

I don't remember how I got out of the store or if I even bought anything. The part I do remember is when I got to my car I called Tom right away. By the time he answered, I was a mess, crying and shaking uncontrollably. I managed to tell him I had gotten the call and I was not a match to Donna. After telling me he was sorry, his next words cut me to the core.

"Did you really expect to be a match?"

What? *Did I really expect to be a match?* Seriously? My crying fit stopped almost immediately! As stunned, and temporarily hurt, as I was, I pulled it together enough to respond, "Well, yes! I didn't go into this not to be a match!"

I now know his question was not meant to hurt, he simply asked the question that everyone else was thinking. He tends to do that from time to time.

I also now realize by the time a person decides to donate a body part to another person, they have pretty much convinced themselves they WILL be a match. Otherwise, why would someone go to the trouble to be tested? If you're hoping you won't be a match, then what's the point?

Telling Donna

The days and weeks after the phone call from UAB Jill were a blur, but I do remember having to muster the courage to tell Donna I was not her match. Something else they don't tell you when you are being tested as a possible donor is that whatever the result of the tests, it is up to the one being tested to tell the recipient the results of the tests. In other words, it was up to me to tell Donna that I was not a match.

I could have chosen not to tell her, but I felt it was only fair to let her know. As I contemplated how to tell her I felt like she was going to be so disappointed in me. It wasn't like I had any control over being a match or not, but still the thought crossed my mind.

I don't remember when or exactly how I told Donna, but I do remember her reaction. She was calm and very reassuring. She assured me it was okay and thanked me for going through the testing process.

The peacefulness she exhibited was amazing. She didn't seem shocked or undeterred by my news. She made me feel like it was okay and thankful for my obedience to God's prompting to go through the testing process in the first place. Her peacefulness put me at ease and the thought of going further in the process started running through my mind even more than before.

I told her I was still thinking about going forward in the process to donate on her behalf, but for whatever reason I just wasn't sure yet. She again reassured me that I should not feel pressured to go further. I didn't feel pressure to go forward, in fact, the thought wouldn't leave me alone.

I felt like it should be an "easy" decision to go forward. Although I wasn't a match for Donna if I decided to donate a kidney on her behalf it would add another person to the pool of possible donors.

This, in turn, would help the hospital find more matches. It could help Donna get a kidney sooner and helping her was the reason I started this donation process in the first place, but for whatever reason I couldn't commit just yet.

The donor coordinator, UAB Jill, had also told me the doctors found blood in my urine and they would need to do more tests to find out where the blood was coming from if I should decide to go forward in the process. This had me a little concerned because I had never been told this before. It was not anything visible to the naked eye, so I wasn't too alarmed. I stored that nugget in the back of my mind, at least for the moment. I would cross that bridge whenever I came to it. No need to worry now.

Turning 50

2014 was also another landmark year for me. I was turning the dreaded 5-0. Fifty years old! How in the world did I get to be half of a century old? Mom always said not to wish my life away because it would be over before I knew it and she was right. Life seemed to crawl as a child and now it was passing at the speed of light.

I had celebrated the completion of my dissertation the year before with a party, so I chose not to celebrate my 50th birthday in a big way. Maybe it was just more about not wanting to recognize how old I really was.

My birthday was June 4th and my sister, Courtney, came in town the following week (Friday, June 13 to be exact) to celebrate my birthday and Father's Day with our dad. Father's Day weekend also marked our dad's high school 61st year class reunion and we had planned to go with him to the event.

Love/Like Relationship

Remember the tat pact I made good on back in March? Well, my parents had not seen my tattoo yet and although Mom was not happy about me getting one, she had not said anything derogatory to me about it. On the other hand, I had no idea what Dad thought about it, but I was about to find out.

You know when people try to figure out which parent you resemble by asking you, "So, who do you look like?" Like *you* are supposed to know who you favor. It's usually someone else who says, "Oh, you look just like your mom/dad/aunt, etc." For whatever reason, we can rarely see our own resemblances.

For years, I had been told I favored my dad and his side of the family. I have, or rather *had,* the family nose. (Confession, I had it surgically "corrected" several years ago.) I was told I had Dad's mouth in appearance as well as the gift of gab. I also have his knees and the family feet. Wide and flat. Dear Lord, yes! Those must have been some dominant genes because both of my kids are cursed with these feet!

So, with so many physical features alike, I can still say I did not always "like" my dad. Not to sound too harsh because I always loved him, but did I *like* him, no, not always. It could be because we were too much alike, or at least that's what my mom and sister tend to say. Maybe because he's male and I'm female. Maybe because we grew up during radically different times. He grew up during the 30s, 40s, and 50s and I during the 60s, 70s, and 80s.

I really can't say.

I can say it was not one particular thing that separated us. As with most family riffs, it was a combination of things over many, many years that probably contributed to our "love from a distance" relationship.

So, on this particular Father's Day weekend

(Friday the 13th should have been our first sign!) we had one of the biggest riffs we had ever had. It was U-G-L-Y! It all started with his disapproval of me getting a tattoo. One thing led to another and I vowed to leave their house. Unfortunately, because it was such a big weekend for the family, Courtney and Mom talked me into staying the night and going to the reunion the following day. Against my better judgment, I stayed.

All the things said that day brought back every horrible thing he had said to me over the years. His expectations were always very high and if I failed to meet those expectations, oh my, well, let's just say when the "D" word (disappointed) got thrown around, you just wanted to pack your bags and run away from home. And those feelings of disappointing my dad all came running back. Just like I was 10 again!

At the end of the weekend, I left my parents' house hurt and emotionally wounded. I wasn't sure we would mend things this time.

Nicest "Firing" I Ever Had

To help with our finances, I worked a part-time job for an online art education company. It had been fun learning how to "teach" online, but it had also been extremely stressful trying to manage a new full-time job and an online teaching load.

Sometime in mid-June I received a call from the owner of the company wanting to talk to me. I knew before she said anything she was letting me go.

It really was one of the nicest firings I had ever been privy to. Not that I've been fired but one other time, but if I had to be let go, I'm glad it happened the way it did. She and I are still good friends and I have great respect for her and her husband and the company they have built.

In reality, she did me a favor. I was burning the candle at both ends and I knew it could not continue much longer. The experience was just what I needed to help me with my full-time job at Troy. I was expected to teach online as part of my course load, but I had never taught an online course before. So, the online teaching experience had been beneficial for learning how to teach in a totally new arena.

Just after the art education company let me go, I heard about a friend leaving her job at the state department. Another art teacher friend contacted me and told me she thought I would be perfect for the job. Well, great! I just made the biggest career change of my life, took a huge pay cut, and now another "dream job" seemed to be opening up. The timing couldn't have been worse!

I debated if I should even pursue the job, but contacted the woman leaving the position and she encouraged me to at least submit my application for an interview. I quickly revamped my vita and submitted it to the state department of education, and then, I waited. And waited some more.

Finally, I got the call for an interview. I was excited, but nervous. Not nervous about the interview or the job, but about the possibility of actually getting an offer and having to decide to leave Troy after only one year.

I loved my new job. It was the sort of job I had dreamed of doing for at least the past 10 years. Would I really give it up after only one year?

Our financial situation was not getting any better and I felt the need to once again supplement our income or to move to a job paying more than what I was currently making. So, in some respects, the job at the state department would solve some of our financial burdens and it would allow me to be home every night.

The interview went really well and I half-hoped they would offer it to me if for nothing else than the money. But, then I thought about it. Why would I change jobs just for the money? Well, I know that sounds like a dumb question, but I had worked for so long to earn my Ph.D. so I could teach at the collegiate level and the state department job would not have any teaching component to it. A lot of politics and administrative work would be the norm and although I was not opposed to either and I knew I could do the job, I still wasn't sure it was really what I wanted to do.

Thankfully the decision was made for me a few weeks later. I didn't get the job, but one of my art teacher friends did. I say "thankfully" because now that he's been in the position for almost four years, I know he was the best person for the job. Hearing about the struggles he deals with on a daily basis I am so glad it's him and not me!

Summer School

June was sort of a blur that summer. I returned to teaching the remainder of June while still contemplating whether or not to go forward in the kidney donation process. I could not bring myself to say "yes", but I wasn't ready to say "no" either. It's like something had a hold of me and would not let go. The thoughts of going forward and helping Donna continued to run through my mind, but nothing had persuaded me to pick up the phone and call UAB Jill to tell her I would go forward.

Life seemed to slip by rather slowly that summer. When I taught elementary school art I had my summers somewhat free, so I had never taught during a summer. This teaching a summer term was new to me. That summer also gave me a lot of alone time. Not only did I have two hours of drive time to Troy and two hours back home every week, but I also house-sat for friends and the empty house forced me to become my own best conversationalist.

The main topic of discussion with myself was always, "Why won't you go forward in the donation process? You already know the only health issue you have is Irritable Bowel Syndrome and you've started making changes to help those issues, so what's holding you back?"

I didn't have an answer. And it seemed no one else did either.

Because I was home on the weekends, I still saw Donna at least every other weekend when I led our greeter group at church. She had stopped serving once her dialysis began, but she would go to church when she was feeling strong enough. On one of those Sundays I told her I still had not made up my mind about going forward in the testing process. She told me something I will never forget. She said, "Kelly, if you're not at peace with your decision, then maybe that's God telling you not to go any further."

Without thinking, I said, "But it won't let go of me!" I tried explaining that when I thought I had made up my mind not to go forward, I was haunted by the thought of not doing it. Haunted is probably not the best word to explain what I was feeling, but the thoughts of going forward and what that could mean for Donna just kept coming back around. I was extremely torn about what to do and I could not figure out why. Then on June 28 I thought my decision had been made for me. I received a phone call from my friend Nicole telling me UAB had found Donna a matching kidney.

In a split second I was elated and saddened all at the same time. I was so thankful Donna was going to have her second chance at life and that UAB had found a match so quickly. I was also saddened that it was not going to be me who helped her get that second chance. A co-worker of Donna's had gone forward in the donation process and agreed to give a kidney on Donna's behalf. This added another person to the pool of potential donor candidates and therefore they were able to find Donna a match pretty darn quick.

I was happy for Donna, but disappointed at the same time. I felt so selfish for even feeling that way and I tried really hard not to let Nicole know how I was feeling. Heck, I wasn't really sure what I was feeling or why! Donna's friend and Donna would have their surgeries on the same day and the date was set for July 17th. Wow! In less than six months, Donna had announced her situation, undergone dialysis, and found a matching kidney. That in itself was a miracle! I have since learned many people may be on dialysis for years and never receive a kidney. It's not for a lack of trying, but some hospitals just don't have the capabilities of connecting donors and recipients like others do. UAB happens to be one of those hospitals that has the capability and they do it very well.

Journal Entry

June 28, 2014:
THANK YOU! Donna has a match and is getting a kidney! So thankful she has a donor! Prayers answered! I'm still struggling with the decision to go forward. Please help me make a decision.

JULY

"My sheep hear my voice, and I know them,
and they follow me."

— JOHN 10:27 (ESV)

Is This Only a Test?

With all of the testing I had undergone over the first half of the year I realized I really needed to get myself in better shape and better health whether I donated a kidney or not. I had spent the past year and a half working full-time, finishing a Ph.D. degree, changing jobs (in another city), and my health had obviously paid the price. I had gained a whopping 20+ pounds and felt sluggish and tired all of the time.

My daughter celebrated her 17th birthday on July 6th and of course we made pictures after dinner that evening. When I got home, and saw the pictures, I cringed! How did I let myself get this big? And why didn't someone tell me?

Well, of course, no one was going to tell me I had gained weight. Some might even justify it with all the stress of me changing jobs, trying to live in two separate towns, our financial issues, etc. They were all a bit *too* nice. Sometimes it just takes *one* image getting posted to social media to spark a change and this was mine. So, on July 7th, I began an exercise regimen and diet for, if nothing else, to regain my energy and feel better overall.

Because I was working the entire summer and had to travel for two professional events, Tom and I were not able to visit his family in Pennsylvania like we had in summers past. He, however, had a class reunion that summer, so he decided he would go up without me.

One afternoon after one of my exercise walks in the southern Alabama heat, we had a Skype call with each other. I was in my office trying to recoup from the heat and exhaustion that comes from starting a new exercise routine in the middle of the summer. Tom was outside at his family's pool enjoying a much less hot day and hanging out with his family.

Somewhere in the conversation, after all the niceties and hearing about each other's week, we turned to my unrelenting struggle to continue in the donation process. Although Donna was scheduled to receive her new kidney within a few days, I was still contemplating the thought of giving to someone else.

Tom asked if I was still thinking about donating. I told him yes, but I didn't know why it was so hard for me to make a decision. He promised he would continue to back me with whatever I decided to do. I thanked him and was truly grateful he had my back through the entire process.

As much as I wanted someone to make the decision for me, he knew it had to be my decision, not his or anyone else's. I have always sought others' "approval" for things I *thought* I was supposed to do or not do. But, in reality, people shouldn't try to be who I or anyone else thinks they should be. We should, however, seek other believers to confirm or refute what we believe God tells us. If things don't line up with His Word, then we're probably not hearing from God.

So far, things seemed to be lining up pretty well. I had listened and began the testing process. I had sought medical advice for my health issues and was doing everything in my power to get healthy and make myself a viable donor candidate. I was praying relentlessly. Tom and I were seeking prayers from our friends and the church. The fact I was still feeling the tug at my heart made me feel like I was supposed to keep going. But was I?

More than once I questioned what this whole thing was really all about. Was it just a test? A test to see if I would in fact listen to God? If I listened, would I actually do what He was telling me to do? And, if I listened and did what He said, would I give Him the credit? That last question was a biggie and would resurface many, many times throughout the year.

Prayers in the Waiting Room

Just when I thought I had done all the tests I could possibly do, I still had more on the calendar. I also needed a mammogram and bone density test to finish all of the OB/GYN tests and for the folks at UAB. I went ahead with the scheduled tests on July

11th, still unsure of whether or not I would go further in the donation process.

I don't really remember anything about that day other than going through the motions. I knew I needed the tests because I was now 50 years old, so I was just doing what I knew had to be done regardless if I was donating a kidney.

I rank the mammogram right behind the annual exam as the most embarrassing test on the planet! Another necessary evil! As I looked around the mammogram waiting area, for the first time I actually looked at the women waiting with me. Most were older than me, maybe a few just a bit younger, but most were absorbed in their own thoughts, their cell phones, or the television playing in the room. No one really spoke to each other. Maybe it was our shared modesty as we went from individuals of all shapes and sizes, colors and ethnicities, and ages, to a common pool of women draped in pink, very unfashionable, hospital gowns. Whatever the reason, I begin to create stories about each of them.

There was an older African-American woman who appeared to be there with her daughter and grandchild. Could she be there for a routine checkup or could it be something more serious? Why would she bring her daughter and grandchild with her?

Moral support? She needed someone to drive her because she doesn't drive?

There was an older Caucasian woman who sat alone and didn't make eye contact with anyone. Did she not have anyone to come with her? Was her appointment a routine one or was there something more going on with her? What if there was? Had she not told anyone? Did she have anyone to tell?

My mind went all over the place as I contemplated a story for each of the women. I could have been totally wrong about each of their stories, but that didn't really matter. I knew one thing I could do that could help each and every one of them. I could pray. And pray I did.

I prayed for all of us in that room. I prayed that whatever the reason we were brought together that day, each of us would be called back quickly and our tests would be painless. I prayed no matter the outcome of our tests God would touch each of our lives with His overwhelming love. I prayed for each of us to be *healed* in whatever way He determined and we would be at peace with the results.

I also prayed for each woman individually for whatever "story" I had penned for them. Through all of this praying, I realized in the midst of *waiting*, I could *do something* for someone else. The women didn't have to know I was doing anything, but maybe my prayers were reaching the Great Physician who really could take away their pain, whether physical, emotional, or spiritual.

Never before had I sat in a waiting room and prayed for the people there with me. If any prayers happened, it was usually only for my doctor to hurry up and get finished with everyone else so he or she could see me. Because when you're in a waiting room full of people it's all about you, right?

My perspective had changed about waiting room protocol after hearing Donna talk about her dialysis and doctor sessions. Sometimes she would have to go to the dialysis center to receive treatments, but most of the time she was able to do them at home. When she was at the center for treatment, she realized she had a lot of time to notice the other people in the room who were hoping for the same miracle as she was: a kidney transplant.

During one of our many conversations that year, she told me she was using her time connected to a machine, to pray for others in the room. Everyone in the room was going through treatments just like her, yet she found a way to pray for them as she endured her own treatments. Some of those people may have been there for a lot longer than she had and she

knew some of them had lost hope of ever receiving a
donor kidney.

So, to take the worry off of herself and her
problems, she decided to pray for others who were
sicker than she was, or at least people she perceived
as being sicker.

Donna's disposition throughout her entire
dilemma was one of peace and understanding. I was
amazed at how she never complained, but rather was
an inspiration to those of us who knew her and a
witness to God's amazing grace to everyone she
came in contact with throughout the year.

On July 17, 2014 Donna's prayers came to
fruition and she received her new kidney.

From January to July she kept saying, "As I walk
closer to Him, He will bless others through me."
Wow! I wanted that kind of relationship with God!
He not only answered her prayers for a new kidney,
but also He touched her spirit in a profound way. In
turn, she witnessed to anyone who would listen
about His love and unending sense of peace.

A Higher Purpose

Tom and I went to visit Donna after church on July
20th. She was still in the hospital, along with her

coworker who had donated on her behalf. Both had surgeries within a day of each other. Donna received a new kidney from a woman in Mississippi and Donna's coworker donated to that woman's mother. Hence, how "donating on behalf of a friend or family member" process works. I still don't really understand how UAB's matching process works, but whatever they do to find kidney matches around the United States is working!

Donna and her co-worker looked amazingly healthy having just gone through major surgeries three days prior. Donna looked so healthy and full of energy. We had not seen that gal in a long time! I've realized after talking to people about their before and after stories, recipients often feel better almost immediately. They are usually so sick prior to the transplant, that once they receive a new kidney, their bodies start working correctly and they feel amazingly better.

Seeing how good both Donna and her coworker looked, I was encouraged about the severity of the surgery and how I might feel afterwards, if I went ahead in the donation process. We talked a little about my still looming decision and once again, Donna tried to reassure me if I wasn't at peace with the decision, then maybe it wasn't God telling me to do it. She also assured me it was okay to not go forward. No one would think any less of me if I didn't.

As much as I think I heard what she said to me, I still could not get it out of my mind and heart. I still did not understand why I couldn't make the decision, one way or the other, but promised Donna I would continue to pray about it.

Several times during this year, I also thought the sole purpose for going through this was just to see if I was actually seeking God above my own ambitions and if I was truly listening to what He was saying to me.

I knew my decision could ultimately save someone's life and I tried to tell myself that's why I needed to keep going forward in the process. If I decided not to go forward, it wasn't so much God telling me not to, but rather, I would feel super guilty and selfish for not continuing. So, then I was back to it being all about me and I knew He did NOT want me focusing on me. This was not about me, although I would be the tool He used to save someone's life, but rather it was about a greater purpose that I could not yet see.

Peace be with You

Shortly after our visit with Donna I traveled to Santa Fe, New Mexico for a National Art Education Association (NAEA) Summer Leadership Conference. At the time, I served as our state's president and as a commissioner on the NAEA Research Commission, so I arrived mid-week, a few days earlier than my president-elect. During those first few days, I was in meetings, but I also had some time to myself to think about what had transpired in my life over the past seven months. I took one day to explore the city and see some art. I located the Museum of Indian Arts and Culture and set out for a day of touring. I saw a lot of art that day and sat, for what seemed like hours, at a restaurant there at the museum. I watched as people, some with their families, some with their spouses, took the day to look at art and enjoy a beautiful day in Santa Fe.

As the families and couples came and went, I thought about the sheer number of people who are in this world and how each one of us could help save the lives of others through something as simple as blood donation or as difficult as an organ donation. What a small price that seemed to be in order to save the life of another.

Recalling how I spent my time that day and the conversation I had with Donna just a few days prior may have been the trigger for me deciding to actually go ahead in the donation process. I do not recall declaring to myself that I was ready to commit to donating, but seeing all those people that day seemed to trigger a response in me. On the last day of the Research Commission's meetings I received a phone call from UAB Jill. As I looked at the phone, I thought, "Uh oh, she's calling for an answer and I'm still not sure what I'm going to say." I excused myself from the meeting to take the call.

As we got through the particulars of seeing how each one of us was doing, she got right to it. "Have you had a chance to talk to your family or think about whether or not you want to go forward in the kidney donation process?", she asked. I hesitated, and then without really thinking about my answer I said, "Yes. Yes, I will go forward." Then, nothing. No response. No comment. No sound. Nothing! I literally thought I had dropped the call! I took the phone off my ear, looked at it, and realized the call was still active. As I was about to say "hello" to see if she was still there she said, "Oh! Okay, well, let's see what you need to do next." In that moment....THE very moment I said, "Yes", all the questioning, all the indecision, and all the wondering left me. I was at complete peace like I had not felt in the past seven months.

Once I realized what I said, UAB Jill continued to tell me I needed to have another test done because they were still finding blood in my urine, but we could talk about it when I got back from Santa Fe. Alrighty, then, if I needed to have another test in order to donate a kidney it really didn't matter at that moment. I was elated! As I walked back into the meeting I looked at one of the board members and said, "I'm going to be a kidney donor!" She appeared shocked and asked, "Really?" The following days were a blur, but I'm sure I told others about my decision. The main thing I do remember was how relaxed and how at peace I was once the decision was made and I said it out loud.

Journal Entry

July 24, 2014: Bless my decision to donate a kidney – now that I've told UAB Hospital I feel relief and peace – I want to do it for the right reasons and not because it will do anything for me – help me to spread Donna's story and Your message!

AUGUST

"For the Lord G*OD* *does nothing without*
revealing his secret to his servants the
prophets."

— A*MOS* 3:7 (ESV)

Clarification

As the reality of what happened in late July
began to sink in I really, I mean REALLY
began to pray. I had been journaling all year, but the
last part of 2014 seemed to be a hyper-focused time
of prayer and journaling.

We've all done this when we face what seems
like a hopeless situation. We tend to pray like crazy

when we experience the death of a loved one, a sick parent or child, or maybe a friend facing divorce. We pray like we've never prayed before. Why is that? To me, it means we're finally desperate. Not desperation like we're giving up, but desperation like we know no one else can handle this burden but our Lord and Savior Jesus Christ.

I had prayed for clarification on whether or not to donate a kidney. I had prayed to be healthy. I had prayed for others to pray for me. I had prayed for my family and friends to support me in this journey. But, now with my decision to go forward and an end goal in mind, my prayers took a turn toward bigger results.

I began to pray about needing clarity and vision for where God wanted to use me next. I had not been approved as a living organ donor and yet I was asking Him where He wanted to use me afterwards! I questioned whether my next assignment was with my group of greeters or another group, or was it in some type of small group either being a participant or leading? Where was I supposed to be: Birmingham, Troy, somewhere else? That's a lot of questions! I obviously had more on my mind and heart than just giving a kidney!

My prayers also turned to a recipient. Although

I had not been approved to be a donor yet, I was thinking positively that I would be. I asked Him to not only find a possible kidney recipient, but also someone who needed salvation. If I could touch someone's spirit with my kidney and my story that could be an awesome testament to His power and His name!

Tom and I were still praying together most mornings and on one particular morning he felt the urging of the Lord to begin praying for a recipient too. He actually prayed *"I was going to blow it off, but obviously, it is something You want us praying for. Thank You for Kelly's heart and ultimately for seeing You through all of this."*

Our prayers shifted from it being all about me to all about a recipient. We prayed like it was really going to happen.

Marriage and Money

I never doubted Tom's conviction towards my desire to give a kidney. He told others if I believed God told me to do this, who was he to question it. Sadly, other parts of our lives and marriage were not so strong.

As I looked back through my journals for snippets of what I was thinking and praying during

2014, I also recalled a lot of hurt. Because I was gone four days a week, our marriage suffered from not living under the same roof most weeks. I had taken a huge cut in my salary to teach at Troy, and Tom was trying to start his own construction business with no working capital. Needless to say, our lives were strained in more ways than one.

I came from a family of arguers. If someone was mad, we knew about it because they would let us know. Tom is not like that.

He's the churning-volcano-ready-to-erupt-at-any-moment type. After three years of marriage, I was still not use to this. I knew when he was upset because he would shut down and not really talk to me, but no amount of coaxing would get him to talk until he erupted.

On the surface, we looked like we were happy and things were going smoothly. Nothing could have been further from the truth. My family argued a lot, but on the outside, we looked like the Beaver Cleavers, but we were not. Arguments about money were especially frequent in our home. In my first marriage, I continued this pattern of making things look "good" while at home arguing continually about children, jobs, and most often, money.

As I prayed for all the issues surrounding my

donation of a kidney, I also prayed for wisdom about
how to handle talking to Tom and about how to "fix"
our money issues. I had asked my parents for money
along the way to help make ends meet, but it was
becoming an almost monthly occurrence and I knew
it could not continue.

In one of my many conversations with my sister,
Courtney, she mentioned a debt consolidation
service one of her colleagues had used. It was called
GreenPath Financial Wellness. Out of desperation I
decided to call them. After a long phone
conversation with one of their debt counselors, I felt
like this was my answer, but it meant I had to get
Tom on the same page about money, and I knew that
would not be easy.

Multiple times I tried showing him we were
getting further and further in debt by trying to keep
his business afloat. He wasn't sure where to get the
working capital needed to keep us and the business
in the black. He dreamed of owning his own
business, so I didn't want to crush his spirit knowing
he was allowing me to pursue my dream of teaching
at the collegiate level.

Tithing to the church was important to both of
us and we were giving but nowhere near the amount
we both thought we should. I couldn't see how we

could give any more when we were struggling with the monthly bills.

After speaking with a debt counselor and setting up a financial plan, I felt much better. Not that we were out of debt, but that we had a plan to deal with the money issues. I'm a gal who needs a plan to know I'm headed somewhere, but God had other "plans" that He didn't think I should be privy to just yet.

Once the debt plan was set up with *GreenPath* we were to pay $650 per month for the next four to four and a half years. Four years?!?! Holy cow, that seemed like a lifetime away!

Getting My Attention

During one of my conversations with UAB Jill she told me the doctors had again found blood in my urine. Still unsure where it was coming from, they wanted me to have yet another test but this time with a urologist.

The events of that visit are a bit fuzzy. I think I've blocked them from my memory! It was one of those "embarrassing" tests I equate to the gynecologist and mammogram visits. Without going into too much detail, hopefully you get the picture. What made it even more embarrassing was the multitude of people in the room with me. I believe there were 7-8 people in the room with me for the test. To this day I still don't know why all those people had to be in the room with me.

When the results came back there seemed to be only one place the blood could be coming from....my kidneys. I thought, "Seriously, how could this be happening?"

Throughout this journey I kept thinking maybe something was wrong with me. Maybe I was going through all of these tests just so doctors would find MY problem. If it was, it seemed like a very strange way to go about discovering my problems, but He had my attention.

Last Option

When UAB Jill told me the very last option would be a kidney biopsy, she explained the procedure was a bit uncomfortable, but it could be done one afternoon and I could return to work within a day or two. She also mentioned I would have to take it easy for three weeks. Three weeks! Wait, what?

No more walking or running for at least three weeks was like telling me not to breathe! I was finally in a running rhythm preparing for my first 5K race in November. The race was the carrot dangling out in front of me enticing me to keep running and losing weight. I had dropped several pounds and was feeling great, so this "don't do anything for three weeks" directive really put a damper on my motivation.

Having spent eight months being poked and prodded I thought, "What's one more test?" Labor Day weekend was coming up, so I scheduled the biopsy for the Friday of that weekend allowing me three days to recover.

The test was my last hope of becoming a kidney donor. UAB Jill informed me that women often have very thin membranes covering their kidneys, so a small amount of blood was normal. If there was too much blood coming from my kidneys, I would not be allowed to donate.

Doubting

A lot of prayers happened the week prior to the biopsy. I prayed for God to give me peace about the procedure. I asked Him to give me clarity for why I was having to jump through so many hoops in order to help someone. I prayed I could accept whatever the results might be. I also prayed for Him to remind me to believe in His will be done and to reveal the purpose in all of what I was going through.

I couldn't understand why I was being led down this path believing He was the one leading me if I wasn't going to give a kidney to someone. What could be the reason for all of these tests and setbacks? I felt like I was wasting time when I could be saving someone's life. Oh....my....goodness! Did I just say that? Holy cow, I did!

It seemed I was having more trouble than most to be cleared for a donation and I was taking it personally. I wanted to donate a kidney to help a friend and when that didn't happen I decided I would help a total stranger. I should get bonus points and an easy ride for that, shouldn't I?

One of the lessons God was obviously trying to show me was some humility. Yes, I wanted to do something wonderful for another one of His children, but I couldn't make it all about me. There were times, usually in private, where I second-guessed myself. Did I really hear God's voice or, was I hearing what I wanted to hear? Was He directing me or was I just looking for the next rung in my proverbial status ladder?

I knew my family would worry about another test and especially one as invasive as a biopsy, but I felt I had to talk to them about it. My dad and I had yet to talk since our huge blow-up in June. Every time I called, I prayed Mom would answer the phone afraid he and I would go at it again. This time I prayed Mom and Dad would be accepting of the news I would be going through another test. They probably all thought I would eventually give up, but the biopsy meant I was serious. The phone call to them, well, Mom, went fine. Naturally, she played devil's advocate and wondered what was wrong with my kidney. I told her the doctors didn't feel like anything was *wrong* with me, just that if my kidneys were leaking too much urine, I could not be considered for donating a kidney.

In late August, I prayed for Him to give me peace about the procedure and make it clear the reason for all of these tests. I said, "I know You will eventually make it all clear," but I wasn't sure He would. Part of me thought it was just one big patience and humility test. Would I go all the way with the tests? Would I actually donate a kidney? Would I tell everyone God told me to do all of this?

I also prayed for God to tell me what I should say to my dad. I still didn't think I had anything to apologize for, but I also knew hell would freeze over before he initiated a reconciliation. Mom and

Courtney continued to tell me I was like my dad, but I did not want to be like him because by golly, I was NOT like him. So, I had to really pray for some words of love and grace.

As the biopsy day grew closer I prayed for a quick and painless procedure, but also for the ability to accept whatever the outcome might be. I continued to pray for clarification because I felt God had led me to do this, but I couldn't figure out why I was having a really hard time donating. I wanted to believe His will was being done and there was a purpose in all of this. I just needed peace and the ability to accept whatever the results might be and move forward.

Biopsy Day

Tom and I showed up early on Friday and the nurse came to get us fairly quickly, then the day came to a grinding halt. I was put in a room with a television and then left alone. When Tom realized, it might be awhile before they actually did my procedure he asked the nurse if it would be okay for him to leave, go check on a job, and come back in a little while. Of course, she said, "Sure! She'll be fine." Thanks, nurse! I was fine, but I was alone, scared, and bored.

Thank goodness there was a television in the room and I had my phone. At least I had some form of entertainment.

Friends and family were texting me to let me know they were praying for me and asking for updates. I honestly don't remember how long I waited for the procedure to start, but it seemed like forever. Unfortunately, Tom did not make it back in time for the procedure, so I prayed for God to go with me into the exam room. What I do remember was the procedure room was small and only the doctor, nurse, and I were in the room because there was little room for anyone else. I was asked to roll over on my stomach. I also remember how uncomfortable that was. I can't remember the last time I laid on my stomach! There were a lot more padding on my tummy than I remember.

The doctor numbed the area of my lower back where they would insert the needle/sword/torture tool into my body. I don't remember his name, but I remember he was super patient and explained everything he did before he did it. Surprisingly, I was able to watch the entire procedure on a small computer screen as he plunged the torture tool into my back.

He even showed me the tiny, and I do mean tiny,

piece of tissue he was extracting from my kidney. The only thing I can equate the procedure to is like when a geologist takes a core sample from the earth. They push a long metal tube into the ground and when they pull it out it will have all the layers from the earth in a compact sequential order. Same thing with a kidney biopsy without the mile-deep plunge, although it felt like it! In the middle of this "interesting" procedure I had to put my face into a pillow I had been hanging on to in order to keep from screaming out loud. They numbed the top layer of my back, but not deep into the muscle close to my kidney. It was painful!

While trying to keep my screams at bay the sweet doctor was trying to distract me by asking me what led up to this test and why I was there. I managed to tell him this was my last hope for donating a kidney. He was intrigued and asked a few more questions. Once when I was trying to control my screams he said, "Makes you wonder if donating a kidney is really worth it, doesn't it?" I know he was trying to be funny and trying to distract me from the pain I was feeling and I did laugh. Unfortunately, they ask you not to move while they are poking and prodding and that included laughing. Seriously? I prayed for a moment of reprieve!

As I began to answer the doctor, I said, "Yeah, well...." And then I stopped. I felt the Holy Spirit say "No pain is too painful when laying down your life for another." I finally mustered enough strength through the pain to say, "No. There is a purpose in all of this." I still wasn't sure what that "purpose" was, but felt the Holy Spirit with me throughout 2014 guiding and directing me toward something. I just didn't know what that "something" was yet, but felt sure it would eventually be revealed. I really had not thought about the pain all of this had caused me. There had not been much physical pain with any of the procedures until now, but there had definitely been emotional and spiritual pain.

There was no way to know what sort of pain my possible recipient could be in or what he/she had dealt with for who knows how long. My one, inconvenient, pseudo-painful procedure was probably nothing compared to what they were going through. I could not imagine the life of someone who needed a kidney and therefore had no right to complain about my momentary discomfort.

Once the procedure was complete I had to go back to the original room I had spent most of the day in and wait. And wait some more. The doctor equated the three samples he just extracted from my left kidney to a scab. My blood would naturally begin clotting to create a scab on the surface of my kidney. If I went running before those holes completely healed, they could open again and bleeding could occur. This bleeding could put me back in the hospital and I did not want that to happen. Ahhhh, all of a sudden I knew why I was not allowed to run for at least three weeks.

More Signs

As I waited for Tom to return and the blood to clot, I again found solace in the television and phone. People had texted all day checking on how I was doing, so I was comforted knowing people were praying for me. I did wonder how many of those people thought I would never be able to donate a kidney. The purpose I thought God called me to fulfill seemed to be slowly slipping away.

With the new small group semester at our church starting soon I decided to search the church's website to find a small group to join in or around Troy. Although this was my second fall semester in Troy I had continued to attend small groups in Birmingham, but it was getting harder to find groups that only met on Thursdays, Fridays, or Saturdays when I would be home. I was curious if there were any Christian running groups in or around Troy, so I typed "Troy, exercise, and women" in the directory's search filter. BAM! The first small group to appear was a Couch to 5K in Troy. Seriously? There was a group that met my every need at the top of the search results? Was this yet another sign I was doing the right thing?

As I read the description, I decided to email the group leader to see if it would be okay to join them but not run for the first few weeks. As I searched for the leader's name and email, again I was stunned. The leader's name was Kelly. Another sign? I emailed her from my hospital bed trying to explain my situation and asked to join the group if only for prayer before their daily run. Not expecting to hear from her until later, I put my phone down and noticed Tom was back. I wasn't feeling very well and just wanted to go home and lay down. By this time, it was dark outside and I realized I had not eaten all day, so we decided to find something close to grab a bite to eat.

We found one of our favorite restaurants, Mooyah Burgers, Fries, and Shakes, and ordered a big ole burger. Tom went to place my order while I squirmed, still in a lot of pain, in a booth checking my messages. I had texted folks who had been checking on me to let them know I was done and heading home. I noticed I also had a new email from the small group leader Kelly.

As I'm reading the email Tom gets to the table. My eyes got big as I read her email response. I looked at Tom and said, "Oh, my goodness! You're not going to believe this!" The small group leader Kelly, said she would love to have me join her small group and there was no problem with just praying and walking for a few weeks. What had me speechless was what she said after that. She shared how she had been dealing with what she thought were kidney issues herself. Was this yet another sign? Was this my purpose in going through all of this? Was He sending me someone who needed help (whether physical or spiritual) or connecting me with others in Troy? I was stoked!!!

I wrote and prayed the next day: *Wow! You work in awesome and wonderful ways! Maybe all this testing and waiting will be worth it. Whether I am supposed to donate or simply support someone else. THERE IS A REASON FOR EVERYTHING! I've gone through all these tests for six months for Your glory – not sure why, but know that I don't have to know why, just that I should obey."*

After that prayer, UAB Jill told me this test was a "last resort" procedure because if they asked people to do this test "first" most would not continue with the process. She was correct! All of the tests up until then had been pretty easy peasy. Draw some blood, take an EKG, pee in a cup, etc. Nothing too invasive and certainly nothing very painful. In retrospect, it was a tolerable pain. I really don't remember it at all. For the next few weeks my back pain would waver between muscle spasms and stiffening. I basically showed up to my classroom, would teach, and then go straight home, take some pain meds, and fall asleep. Although I couldn't wait to get back to running, there was no physical way in heaven I could run during those three weeks.

Journal Entry

August 31, 2014:
Just prayed that all of the tests I've gone through for the past six months will be for His glory. I'm not sure why I'm having to go through all of this, but I also know that I don't have to know, just that I should obey.

SEPTEMBER

"Therefore, I tell you, whatever you ask in prayer, believe that you have received it, and it will be yours."

— Mark 11:25 (NIV)

Ta-Da!

Then, on September 3, just five days after the biopsy, it happened.... I found out I was approved to be a kidney donor!!!!!

The words I thought I would never hear finally rang through the phone from UAB Jill. She relayed a message that the doctors were impressed I would go through the painful biopsy procedure and agreed to let me donate. I'm assuming my kidney membrane was, in fact, not too thin otherwise they would not have agreed to let me be a donor. All I heard was, *"You've been approved to donate a kidney."*

UAB Jill told me they would begin the process of finding a match for my kidney. There was no way to predict when that might be, but she would be in touch.

The emotions I felt were beyond elation! I had waited almost eight months to hear those words – "You have been approved to donate a kidney" – and the day had finally arrived.

Different Kind of Prayers

Immediately my prayers went from praying for God to direct my steps to praying for a recipient. I asked God to find a person who needed a kidney and for someone who needed to hear from Him. I also prayed they would see Him through me.

Although I went into this whole thing to help a friend, my focus had really been on me throughout the process. Granted, I was seeking direction and purpose for myself, but I had forgotten about who might be on the receiving end of this gift.

As I was in the process of writing this book I was

curious what I was actually feeling that day, so I
went back and found my Facebook post from
September 3:

I am ecstatic right now!!!!! I HAVE BEEN
APPROVED AS A KIDNEY DONOR!!!!!! Words
cannot express how overjoyed I am right now. I began
this process 7 months ago when my dear
friend, Donna, told me she needed a kidney and God
spoke to me saying, "Well, you have two" (duh!), so I
decided to give one away. All of the prodding, poking,
& testing have been so worth it. I will not be giving a
kidney to Donna, but I am already praying for the
person who needs my kidney to be found.

I do not have details yet, but I have asked that
when they do find a match the surgery be scheduled
for December. That's the good thing about being the
"donor", you get to choose WHEN it happens! Plus,
that would give me more time to heal over the
Christmas holiday break from teaching and possibly
not miss any work.

This is a scripture I have referred to often during
many life challenges/trials, so I thought I would
share it.

1 Peter 1:6-7 (NLV)
"So be truly glad. There is wonderful joy ahead,

even though you have to endure many trials for a little while. These trials will show that your faith is genuine. It is being tested as fire test and purifies gold —though your faith remains strong through many trials, it will bring you much praise and glory and honor on the day when Jesus Christ is revealed to the whole world."

Thank you for everyone who has been praying for me during this entire time! Love you all!

It had truly been a long process and there were times I began to doubt it would ever happen, but reading back through my Facebook post I remember the excitement I felt that day all over again. I was getting anxious and wanted to make things go at my pace when I knew full well it all had to be at God's pace.

God was finally making things happen, for whatever reason, eight months later and I was beyond happy.

Giving Him 100% Credit

As I continued to pray for a recipient, people with kidney issues or people who had donated a kidney just kept appearing in my life. The other Kelly in

Troy was one, and then an unexpected one from New York. A colleague of mine told me she was listening to National Public Radio (NPR) and heard a woman talking about her altruistic kidney donation. She felt the same urgings I had felt and made the decision to voluntarily donate a kidney to a complete stranger. I did a little research and found her on Facebook. Thank goodness for Facebook! Her name was Angela and she gave me some great inside information on the good, the bad, and the ugly of organ donation. I knew this wouldn't be all fun and games, so it was great to have someone tell me the stuff you don't read about on websites.

On the way back to Birmingham one Thursday afternoon I was thinking about everything that had happened since January and was just amazed. Just a year ago I could not have imagined I would be teaching at a college AND getting ready to donate a kidney. Okay, I could imagine teaching at the collegiate level because that had been my dream for a long time, but giving a kidney? No way!

I began to wonder what I would say to people if they asked me, "did you really hear God tell you to donate a kidney?" Thinking about what I would say, I thought I would most likely say, "Well, I'm 99.9......" and again, I was interrupted! I heard the

Holy Spirit in a rather snarky tone, say, *"If you can't give me 100% of the credit, then there is no reason to do any of this!"* Just like in my room eight months ago, I looked around to see if someone was in the car with me because it came through so clearly. Nope. Again, I was alone, but just like back in February, I heard God's voice as clear as a bell!

I immediately said, "Okay! I'll give you 100% of the credit for ALL of this! Even if, in the end, I cannot donate a kidney, I will tell everyone, who will listen, that YOU told me to do this." Again, another sense of peace fell over me. I still didn't know if I would have a recipient any time soon, but I felt confident I was doing what God wanted me to do.

Do Not Accept "Man's" Explanation

For the first few weeks of September I tried to go about my days without worrying when I would be matched with a recipient, but I was beginning to get anxious. This part of the journey was out of my control, but I still wanted to make it happen NOW. I had my "plan" of how things were supposed to happen and I wasn't sure any of it was going to work out the way I had hoped.

My plan was to finish the semester, donate a

kidney, enjoy Christmas, and be back teaching in January when the spring semester started. I was still a newbie at Troy University and didn't want to run the risk of asking off for "extra" time during a semester, no matter how noble the cause.

Tom left on September 13 for a 10-day trip to Chile where he worked with some missionary friends from the bible college he had attended. I thought it was good that he would be gone for a little while so I could catch up with work stuff and try to get ahead, just in case "my plan" came to fruition. Unfortunately, his absence also gave me a lot of time to think and ponder what could possibly happen over the next few months. I tried not to think too much about the scheduling of surgery, the possible recipient, or how my schedule could be worked out, but of course, being a planner and worrier I did just that. I over-thought it all.

Then, on September 19 I received THE call that changed my life's trajectory forever. UAB Jill called to say they might have a match for me. They said they were continuing to check the blood of EIGHT people (4 donors and 4 recipients) to make sure our blood was compatible with our possible matches. This meant there could be FOUR transplants in one day!

I was elated and wanted to jump up and down screaming with excitement, but I tried to stay focused to hear what UAB Jill was trying to tell me. One thing I did ask was, "So, do I remember you saying the donor can pick the date of the surgery? Is that correct?" UAB Jill's reaction to my question was sort of funny. She said, "Oh, yes! If you're donating body parts, you get to pick any day you want!" I quickly looked at my calendar and decided on Thursday, December 11th.

If the hospital could work out doing the surgeries on December 11 I could finish my classes a bit early, be home a day to clean and pack, and then get to the hospital late Wednesday or early Thursday. Well, that didn't work out quite like I planned.

As the month of September progressed I continued to hear from people who either knew someone who had kidney issues or who knew someone who had donated. These stories from others helped me see how He really wanted me to do this and to be a light for Him.

Because Tom was still in Chile I texted him the news about the hospital finding a recipient. We were able to talk occasionally and during one of our conversations, we prayed together. Tom prayed, "Thank you for bringing this kidney thing into clarity and for the surgery and recovery that are to come. Thank you for continuing to show Kelly that this is what You want her to do. Don't allow her to accept 'man's' explanation for all of this – It's all You – let her give you all the Glory! We pray for others to know You by this donation and to see Your name magnified."

I loved that he said, "Don't allow her to accept 'man's' explanation for all of this." Tom was right; I couldn't let what others said to me about what I had gone through for months deter me. All of the things that had happened, all the things that were happening, and all the things that would happen could possibly be explained through the lens of man, but Tom and I chose to believe God had His hand in EVERYTHING during this journey.

Ways of Communicating

As I started my two-hour drive home on September 25th, I called my mom like I did every Thursday. We talked about life in general and then we started talking about how we often hear from God in the strangest ways (through others, in snarky snippets, soft whispers, vivid images, etc.). Mom said, "Ya know, I think He speaks to us in ways we will listen. Maybe a whisper works for some, but maybe a snarky, sarcastic voice is what gets your attention." I had to agree with her. Not that I had experienced many "encounters" with God, or at least I didn't think I had, but I did recognize when things were "different." Those different moments caught my attention and caused me to listen.

After Mom and I finished our phone conversation, I turned my car radio to 93.7 WDJC-FM, a local Christian radio station in Birmingham. Ironically, or maybe purposefully, the afternoon program DJs were talking about the very same thing Mom and I had just discussed: How do you know when God is speaking to you?

I gasped and smiled up toward where I imagined God was looking down at me. I exclaimed, "Are you kidding me?" I knew I had to try calling in to the station. I called and one of the radio personalities answered the phone. A bit taken aback because I couldn't tell if we were live or not, I stumbled to verbalize what I wanted to say. Because I had literally just finished a conversation with Mom and made a knee-jerk reaction to call the radio station, my story wasn't fully formed. I remember being able

to fumble around to tell them I had just gotten off
the phone with my mother talking about the same
thing and that I believed God had told me to become
a living organ donor. They both said, "Wow! You're
going to give a kidney to someone? That's awesome!"
When they realized, I was giving to a stranger, they
became even more intrigued. I was somehow able to
consolidate my eight-month ordeal into a matter of
minutes.

When we finished, I quickly texted Tom to see if
he was home after work. I told him to turn his
phone's Tune-In app to WDJC and listen. The
conversation had not been live, but recorded and the
DJs would play it back after the commercial break. I
was again dumbfounded by how God continued to
show me I was truly doing what He wanted me to
do. He uses whatever kind of communication tool
He can to get us to listen, just like Mom said.

ReCreate Conference

The following day, September 26, I had to go to the
hospital for more blood-work. The nurses took five
more vials from me and then I was back to the
waiting game. I thought they continued to have me

doing blood-work because all eight of the possible kidney donors and recipients had to "match" or at least be compatible. I have O+ blood, so I knew I could "match" any blood type, but I didn't understand why I had to continue to have blood drawn. God would make all of this clear in the coming months.

I was looking forward to the weekend and one of my favorite conferences, the ReCreate Women's Conference, at Church of the Highlands in Birmingham. The conference is a great time to spend with girlfriends, relax, rejoice, and rejuvenate.

The lineup was superb, as always, with Meredith Andrews and Highlands Worship providing glorious music, and guest speakers, Holly Wagner and Julia A'Bell, provided the crowd with uplifting and challenging messages. I knew there was a reason I had to go that year. Guess what both Holly Wagner and Julia A'Bell spoke on? Getting out of our comfort zones, learning new things, doing new things, stretching ourselves, and walking into something new that God has planned for us. Wow! Spot on messages that I needed to hear.

Both talked about how stretching ourselves and growing are never the easy part, yet they are probably the hardest part when doing something new. Stretching our wings in order to fly into whatever it is God has for us is many times painful and uncomfortable. Occasionally, those times of growth can seem unbearable, but are usually necessary if we truly want to live a God-led life.

Julia A'Bell's message talked about walking into something new that God has planned for us and to do it confidently. I was certainly walking into something new, but I wasn't sure I was going into it with a lot of confidence.

Weird Dream

Within this rejuvenating and inspiring weekend, I also had one very weird and very vivid dream. I dreamed I was witnessing my kidney surgery as an outer body experience. I was hovering above the operating table and as the surgeon extracted my kidney, he dropped it on the floor! I had an overwhelming feeling of needing to help in some way, but I couldn't. I'm no dream whisperer, so who knows what it really meant, if anything. I woke somewhat worried, but realized maybe it was about me trying to control everything on this journey and I couldn't, nor was I supposed to. I also wondered if this was God's way of assuring me He was in charge?

Journal Entry

September 16 ,2014: I know it's You when my mind is headed in a stream of consciousness and I hear a short, quick response, that is CLEAR!

OCTOBER

"Finally, all of you, have unity of mind,
sympathy, brotherly love, a tender heart,
and a humble mind."

— 1 PETER 3:8 (NIV)

Camping Trip

During the first weekend in October I tried to surprise Tom with a camping trip. I say "tried" because he put all of my clues together and figured out what I was up to. It was probably a good thing he did because he thought of stuff to take with us that I had not thought about, so he actually made the trip a bit more enjoyable. The year had brought us a lot of strife and I wanted to see if getting away from home and our normal routine for a few days might help.

We didn't really have the money to spend on a hotel room, but I was able to purchase a small tent and a few camping essentials so we could camp at a local state park for very cheap. Their "primitive" camping spots were just that—primitive. There was no water and no electricity. There was just a fire pit and an area to pitch a tent.

Unfortunately, our "small" tent was also just that—small! The inflatable mattress we brought would not fit inside the tent, so we ended up sleeping in the very small tent with sleeping bags on top of a very lumpy and hard ground. As we looked at the other campers around us, we realized most were in RVs or much larger tents than ours. Everyone else's tents made ours look like a pup tent!

We spent the weekend napping in hammocks, riding our mountain bikes, going for long walks, and just talking, something we had not done in quite some time. I wrote in my journal that weekend: *I feel so at peace right now – the sounds of God's creations are music to my ears!*

Time to Bury the Hatchet

As the date of surgery grew ever more probable the
Holy Spirit starting nudging me to bury the hatchet
with Dad before my surgery. I wasn't sure why. Was
something going to happen to me? Was something
going to happen to him?

I've had multiple surgeries in my lifetime and
obviously survived them all, so the fear of surgery
actually did not bother me. Many people asked me
about the fear of going under the knife, but honestly,
that was never a concern of mine. Granted, I knew
the risks of any surgery, but those risks never affected
my decision to donate. I called Mom and told her
Tom and I wanted to drive to their house after
church one Sunday so Dad and I could talk and
hopefully mend our relationship. I was anxious,
worried, and nervous to confront him about what
was said back in May. The words my dad said to me,
in front of my husband and daughter were hurtful
and unnecessary, but I already knew he would say
he was just speaking "the truth" as he saw it.

I usually don't handle any sort of confrontation
very well, so I first wrote out what I really wanted to
say to Dad. I laid out the key points I wanted to
make and then wrote supporting points to solidify

everything. Writing an argument is one thing, but saying it with the same attitude and meaning was a whole different ball game. I had a history of getting emotional when talking to my dad, so I was trying to run through every possible comeback he might have so I could keep my emotions intact. Before Tom and I left, I asked my church small group to pray for me. I knew I would need all the help I could get before I tried to talk to Dad. I wanted to talk to him by myself, so neither Mom, nor Tom would be in the room to support me. I prayed for God to be beside me through the entire ordeal. I knew God could use this situation for good because He was using everything in this journey for good.

As we started the hour and a half drive to Mom and Dad's I read the letter I had written to my dad to Tom asking for his feedback. He said everything I wrote in the letter was "true" but he suggested not saying everything or at least not in the way I had written it. I knew he was correct even though I really wanted to say ALL of those things. I decided I would try my best to be gracious and respectful. When we got to Mom and Dad's we did our normal greetings and then I went out to the porch where Dad liked to watch TV and nap. I shared with him that I wasn't sure why I was feeling the urge to talk to him before my surgery, but I wanted to try and clear the air about what happened in June.

He let me talk first and I explained why I was so upset with the way he had reacted to my tattoo, the things he said in front of Tom and my daughter. He shared he had not thought that much about our argument. He did apologize for hurting my feelings, but said he was only speaking the "truth" as he saw it. I realized I couldn't change what he considered as "truth" and decided not to let it go without me saying, "Dad, all things, truth or not, do not need to be said." I really don't think he ever understood how hurtful his "truthful" statements could be. He just saw it as a true statement, therefore it could and should be said. We talked a lot about his beliefs on tattoos and his dismay at why I was wearing mine with pride. He equated tattoos with military guys from long ago and did not see the sentiment I saw in mine. We agreed to disagree on that one.

One of the other topics that came up was Tom and my money issues. I still felt ashamed of our money problems and the fact that he and Mom had helped us out on countless occasions in the past few years. I really didn't want to have that conversation, but we did. He offered to get us out of the debt we were currently in, but I said no. I told him I didn't think we would learn anything from it if he paid our way out. He told me that was a very mature way to think and he appreciated me standing up for myself.

My dad's financial help always seemed to come with some sort of stipulation and that was a point of contention between my ex-husband, Dad, and myself. I decided to turn down Dad's financial offer because I truly believed we needed to get ourselves out of this mess and I refused to be tied to his guilt trips about money any longer. It may have taken me 50 years to get to that point and to stand up to my dad, but I was bound and determined to do it.

No Regrets

By the end of the conversation with my dad much of the bitterness had subsided and I was so grateful. I thanked God for giving me the courage to stand up to him about money and to talk to him without getting emotional. It felt like God was literally sitting right next to me instructing me about what to say when Dad would come at me with something. It was probably one of the most loving and successful conversations I ever had with my dad.

Another topic of our discussion was the fact that he never calls my sister, Courtney or me; it was always us calling him. He surprised me the next morning by calling and saying he wasn't too old to learn something new. He said he would call Courtney and me once a week just to say "hello." Wow! That was huge! He did keep this up for a while. He would mostly text, but it was still great for him to at least try to stay in touch with us.

Once Dad and I finished our conversation, I felt much better about things. I still wasn't completely satisfied he truly understood my position about things, but he probably thought the same of me. We ended the discussion telling each we loved the other one and things were good between us. I knew I could go forward in the kidney donation process with a clear conscious. If anything happened to me, all was well with my soul and I could leave this earth knowing I had no regrets. By the end of October, we found out my dad would have a biopsy of his prostate causing me some worry, yet peace knowing we had made things good between us no matter what the outcome of the biopsy.

Digging in with Prayer

As my dad and I cleared the air and October came to a close, I still had several things bothering me. One thing I was contemplating was when to step down as a greeter team leader at our church. I loved leading the group of greeters I had served with for several years, but it was getting harder and harder to be 100% present on the weekends when I was in town. I was exhausted from still trying to learn a new job and keeping my home life (marriage and motherhood) intact, so I knew I had to give up something and soon. I prayed for God to show me when and how to step down from my leadership position.

I was also praying for my kidney recipient. Even though I wanted to choose the date of the surgery I started thinking, "What if the recipient needs a kidney before December 11? Would I possibly be putting someone's life in jeopardy simply by delaying the surgery?" Again, God was reminding me this whole thing was not about me, but yet about someone who needed a life-saving miracle this year. I continued to pray for the recipient and me to remain healthy until December 11. I also prayed for the other six surgeries to go well and to have no complications. I prayed that everyone involved would be people who needed a ray of hope and that my kidney, along with the other donors', would be the vessels allowing God into their lives in a big way.

Another area on my mind in October was the church small groups in Troy. I felt people were looking to me to begin leading small groups. I had routinely been asked to pray, to share stories, and to be part of the planning team for the next semester. During times of small group worship, I caught myself thinking, "Lord, I don't know if I'm ready for this next step." On several occasions, I heard Him say, "I would not have brought you here if I didn't think you were ready, so go ahead and I will equip you." I prayed for God to put a group on my heart and to truly equip me to lead a small group in Troy.

Money issues were really on my mind during October as well. I honestly didn't know how we were going to provide for Christmas that year. I continued to pray and thank God for everything we HAD so I would stop worrying about what we DIDN'T have. I considered taking another part-time job, but I wasn't sure how to manage it with traveling and teaching full-time in Troy. I think I was embarrassed, sad, frustrated, stressed, and anxious about the entire mess. I prayed for God to take this burden away, but just like with my dad, I knew if God supernaturally made our debt disappear we would never learn how to manage money going forward. I prayed for God to help Tom and I see how we were mismanaging our money and how to get out of debt with the debt consolidation company I contacted in August.

I knew financial issues were really bothering me when I started dreaming about it and woke one morning to Casting Crowns' *Praise You in This Storm*. How appropriate! I knew our money issues were the present storms in our lives. I knew in my head I needed to let go, stop worrying, and trust Him more, but my emotions wouldn't let me.

A Year of Surgeries

Not only was 2014 a year of kidney surgeries for Donna and myself, but other friends had shoulder surgeries, nasal surgery, etc. and my dad had a biopsy of his prostate. One of the most frightening surgeries was that of one of my greeters, Karen. Karen's family had a history of breast cancer and she knew she was probably in line to face the same battle. She had gone through the genetic testing and I believe a biopsy, and decided a complete mastectomy was the best decision to combat the deadly disease. She had her bilateral mastectomy on October 28th and the surgery was a complete success.

Karen's surgery, along with Donna's, had me

thinking a lot about life and death during 2014. Why do people get sick? Why do we have to die? Why is life so hard? Seeing people who were living fulfilling lives, dedicating themselves to the church, their families, and friends, and who appeared to have a long life ahead of them. Why? Why should those people be the ones to get sick? The fact I was the relatively "healthy" one preparing for a surgery to help someone else was a rather odd position to be in. Why me? Why had I for the majority of my life been fairly healthy? How did I get to be the healthy one? Was my health, even with all the sinful things I had done in my life, the reason I was put on this earth?

Journal Entry

October 22, 2014: I continue to pray for my surgery in December, along with the possible seven other surgeries. We ask that all the surgeries go smoothly and with no complications. I pray my recipient will be someone who needs a ray of hope, a new kidney, and to hear from You. Allow my kidney to be the vessel that allows You into their lives in a big way.

NOVEMBER

"Count it all joy, my brothers, when you meet trials of various kinds, for you know that the testing of your faith produces steadfastness. And let steadfastness have its full effect, that you may be perfect and complete, lacking in nothing."

— JAMES 1:2-4 (ESV)

Rollercoaster of Emotions

November brought about several good moments and several not-so-good moments. It really was a month of extreme highs and lows. I was part of our church's small groups in Troy that cooked dinner every week for the college students who attended the group. During the first week of November I decided not to attend the group meeting to catch up on things for work and stay ahead of the game so finishing the semester would go smoothly. I was responsible for part of the meal that evening, so I thought I could run it over to the small group, say my apologies, and be on my way. Well, the Enemy had other plans.

As I approached downtown Troy I noticed a car waiting to pull out of an apartment complex. Getting closer I could see the girl was looking to her right, but not her left (the direction I was coming from). I started muttering, "Don't do it! No, no, no!" But, you guessed it, she did it. She pulled out just in time to clip the right front of my car. Thankfully I wasn't going very fast, so I was able to control the car across the road and stop safely on the sidewalk just shy of a light pole.

I had my wits about myself enough to grab the phone and call 911. As the emergency operator started asking me questions I was outside the car looking to cross the road to the young girl who was obviously shaken. She was crying and saying she was sorry. I asked if she was okay and she shook her head yes. I was trying to tell the emergency operator where we were located and the young girl was able to help me out with directions.

Being that we were literally two blocks from the police station a police officer was on the spot rather quickly. He asked us to move our cars into the apartment parking lot and off the street. As I moved my car I realized something was severely wrong with it. The girl who hit me bent the front bumper and the area around my tire, so it was scraping the tire as it moved.

Realizing I was not going to make it to small group, nor could I drive the car anywhere, I called one of the small group leaders who just happened to be our insurance agent as well. He too arrived quickly and started instructing me on taking pictures of my car, etc. As I talked to the young girl and police officer, I found out she was a student at Troy University who was on her way to class. She was visibly shaken and I tried to reassure her it would be okay.

Of course, the joke became this is what can happen to you when you don't attend small group every week. Although all worked out that night, I was worried about the car and how I would get around the next few weeks. We were planning to head north to spend Thanksgiving with Tom's

parents since I could not travel in December after
my surgery. Looking back, I see where the Enemy
was again trying to derail me from life in general. He
was looking for anything to throw me off my game.
He seemed to have prolonged my ability to make a
decision to go forward in the kidney donation
process, he got me frustrated with all the tests I had
to withstand, and now he was literally throwing me
into chaos with transportation and plans for the
holidays. If my job was located where I lived, it
would have been one thing, but living and working
in separate towns was going to make traveling a bit
more difficult.

Tom came to Troy the next day to help me deal
with insurance and car rental issues. Thankfully our
insurance company paid for a rental car until we
could find out more about the girl's insurance
coverage and what would happen to my car. I was
secretly hoping they would total out my car. Annie
Acura, as I affectionately called her, had been a great
car for almost 10 years, but she was pushing 200,000
miles and wearing out quickly.

Conference News

I was able to get a rental car fairly quickly which freed me to drive back and forth to work and get me through the next few weeks. Our Alabama Art Education Association's annual conference was scheduled for November in our state's capital city, Montgomery. Being the president, I had some major responsibilities at the conference, so I had to be there. Part of me wanted to just stay home and relax after a very crazy beginning to November. I had brought in the keynote speaker, Jessica Balsley, who had been my former boss from The Art of Education, so again, I had too much responsibility to miss this conference.

Jessica had offered to not only be our keynote speaker, but she would also lead workshops. While waiting for her workshops to begin, she and I were sitting at the conference registration table catching up with each other when I got a call from Mom. Dad's biopsy results had come back positive for CANCER. The "C" word no one wants to ever hear.

Although not a total surprise, it was still a shock to hear and I could tell from Mom's voice she was shaken as well. I remember her saying they would have to begin talks with Dad's doctors about forms of treatment, so she didn't have much else to tell me other than the bad news of cancer. She did say Dad was in good spirits and ready to face whatever was to come next.

The art education conference came to an end with everyone enjoying a weekend away from teaching and seeing friends that we only get to see once a year. Jessica and others around me that day were very compassionate and offered to pray for me and my family. It's always good to have your buddies around when receiving bad news and my art buddies have rarely let me down.

First Thanksgiving with Snow

With two bummer events in November—the car accident and Dad's cancer news— it took everything I had to stay focused on finishing the semester and praying for my kidney recipient. Although some things may have gone by the wayside or diverted my attention during November, I made sure to pray every day for those involved in our upcoming surgeries. I prayed for myself and my recipient, the others involved in surgeries that day, as well as all of the doctors and nurses we had yet to meet.

By the time Thanksgiving/fall break rolled around my car was still not repaired. The insurance company did not say my car was totaled, so that meant we had to have it repaired in Troy or have it towed back to Birmingham. Because towing it would probably have been our expense, we decided to have the work done in Troy by someone recommended to us. And, due to the holidays, the local car repair shop could not get the parts in before we left for Pennsylvania, so we were distracted by yet another bump in the road.

We had decided we would go to Tom's parents for Thanksgiving instead of Christmas which had been our tradition for the past four years. We rotated Christmases with his family and mine each year and this should have been the year we had Christmas with the Tom's family. So, on top of dealing with a wrecked car and news my dad had cancer, I also had to get Christmas shopping done by the time we left in late November. Fortunately, Tom is a good shopper and took care of some of the shopping while I was away in Troy.

We usually drove our car to Pennsylvania so we could take our chocolate Labrador Retriever, Lucy, with us, so on this particular trip we had to drive a rental car. We received permission to drive the rental car that far due to the fact we had the trip planned way before the accident happened. Although we technically weren't supposed to have an animal in the rental car, we won't tell anyone if you won't.

The trip is always a long one, but that year seemed to be fairly easy. We were able to see both sides of Tom's extended families and spend quality time with his parents, sister, brother-in-law, and nieces. And, it snowed! I had rarely ever seen snow since I was born a Southern gal, so to see it at Thanksgiving was a bonus.

As I reflected on all the things that happened in 2014, I was amazed. It had been a wild and crazy ride and I was about to do something I never imagined myself doing—donating a kidney to a stranger. I journaled about how enjoyable our visit had been but also how much I "hated 2014" when it came to money issues. It had been an exceptionally hard year as far as finances and I wasn't sure things would get any better in 2015. I prayed for either something to happened with Tom's business (like an investor) or he would decide running his own business was not for him.

As we drove the long drive home, I thought things seemed peaceful, happy, and upbeat, or so I thought.....

Journal Entry

November 4, 2014: Bless my tongue with good things. I apologize for the things I said to Tom this weekend about money. I am so worried about how we will pay bills and how we are not on the same page when it comes to finances. Please help us to work together in order to get out of debt.

DECEMBER

*"Greater love has no one than this: to lay
down one's life for one's friends."*

— John 15:13 (NIV)

What the What?

After coming off an emotional month like
November and trying to wrap up a semester
earlier than usual in order to get home to prepare for
surgery, I was spent. I needed all of my exams to be
finished and all of my grading done and reported in
order to leave Troy for the winter break. I was
focused on what had to get done in a short amount of
time in order to make it home by December 10th.

The students had been wonderful about
everything. Once I knew the surgery had a
scheduled date, I told them what I needed to do in
order to be done a few days earlier than usual. Most
were overjoyed to be done early so they could focus
on other classes and finals, so it worked out great for
everyone. Some even shared with me that they
would be praying for me and wished me well.

At the same time, Tom was working out of town
for a few weeks. He had to pass through Troy on his
way to a beach house he was working on, and I had
asked him to bring me something I had forgotten
from home. He dropped by my office on his way
through and I met him at his truck. He was acting
rather short with me, but I wasn't sure why. I
thanked him for bringing me my stuff and wished
him well as he worked that week. I went to kiss him
and he turned from me. He mumbled something and
I when asked what he said he firmly said, "I'm tired
of everything!" When I asked what that meant he
again brushed me off, jumped in his truck, and blew
out of the parking lot. I was dumbfounded. What
was going on? Did I miss a clue of something I had
done or said to him? I really wasn't sure.

I didn't hear from him the rest of the day and I
don't know if I tried to text him or not. We had only

been married just over three years and we had not experienced many fights, but this often happened when we did have a "tiff." He wouldn't talk, text, or call until I forced him into talking to me.

After I didn't hear from him for a day or two, I asked him to call me. Well, he called, and we talked, but man, was it a doozy. One thing led to another and before I knew it he was asking for a divorce. What the what? Seriously? We just came off a great trip visiting his family, I'm eight days away from a major surgery, and he hits me with the D-word! I was devastated.

We fought about money, living apart, his negativity, me putting him down, and the surgery date (although I do not remember what it was about the date that was so controversial). It was bad. I mean, it was REALLY bad. I cried like I had never cried with him before. I knew things weren't perfect, but I still loved him with all my heart and divorce was not anywhere on my radar. I did think something was going to have to change, but I had not been willing to think about it or face it until after my surgery.

I now see where, yet again, the Enemy was doing everything in his power to separate us as a couple and to maybe even stop the surgery from happening.

I had been torn apart and beaten down in my first marriage from constant arguing and I was determined not to let that happen again, but I wasn't sure I had a choice in this situation.

Tom and I argued about other things like him doing a LIFE group (one of the church's intensive small group structured to deal with life's baggage), and my kids. After a lot of screaming and crying, we both calmed down and he agreed to seek marriage counseling after the holidays.

Because he was working out of town, we did not see each other until Saturday when he returned to Birmingham. Not really talking to him all week except via a few texts here and there, I wasn't sure what to expect when he got home. Surprisingly, he showed up with flowers and a sweet card. We apologized to each other, cried, and genuinely had a nice evening with each other.

As great as that "kiss and make-up" weekend was, I was still scared Tom was planning to leave. The Enemy convinced me that I would probably go through with the surgery, but I was still going to lose my husband. He whispered if I lost Tom and went through another divorce, the problem was obviously me and I would be branded a total loser. Inside I was scared to death, but I wouldn't let anyone know.

Stepping Down

After much consideration, I made the decision Sunday, December 7th would be my last day leading our greeter group, but had only told my co-leader, Lee, and our Dream Team Leader, Nicole. I made bookmarks for all of the greeters with a special scripture on the back and prepared to give my last "sermonette."

It was much harder than I thought it would be. I had served with some of those folks since I came to the church, so it was emotional for all of us. Tom came to support me and to hear me say my good-byes. I cried, he cried, and some of the greeters cried. Most of them knew about my decision to donate a kidney, so I shared my thoughts on being led elsewhere. I knew God had been leading me all year into something new, but I still wasn't sure what that was.

As hard as it was to say good-bye, it felt right and I was again at peace with life.

Godly Counsel

After Tom and my knock-down-drag-out earlier in the month, I called one of my dear friends and fellow greeters, Janet. I had talked to her about our horrible argument and asked if she and her husband, Mac, might be willing to talk with us. They both came from divorced situations and had shared with us some of the same struggles concerning marriage, blended families, and money. Mac co-led one of the usher teams with Tom, so I felt like Tom would be willing to talk with them about our issues.

Mac contacted Tom about having lunch on Sunday after church and Tom graciously agreed. I'm not sure who asked Tom to talk to Mac and Janet about marriage issues, but one of us did and Tom was willing to listen. I was SO thankful! If I've learned anything with a second marriage, kids, or bosses it's to let someone else suggest an idea when they're put out with you so they are much more receptive to being a part of the conversation.

I had prayed all week that Tom would stay receptive to the conversation and that we both would talk with our hearts and not just our emotions. We did talk to them about being divorced, blended families, and money issues and their suggestions were invaluable. We gleaned so much from them in the two hours we spent together. The biggest thing they said to us right off the bat was to take divorce off the table. If we truly loved each other, then divorce couldn't be an option. If we truly loved each other, then all the other stuff would work itself out.

We thanked them and promised we would seek further counseling from the pastor who had married us just three years prior. It was not going to be easy, but if we were both willing to work at it, I felt confident we would make this marriage work. I felt the enemy's voice getting smaller and smaller.

The Countdown Begins

After the emotional rollercoaster of the past week, I still had to return to Troy for two days. I needed to finish grades and wrap up things at the office, so I begrudgingly drove back.

My car was still not finished being repaired, but luckily my housemates offered their car to drive back to Birmingham with the plan for them to pick up my car and bring it to Birmingham later that week.

I had to go for more blood work on Monday at the local hospital in Troy. I had gone for blood work so many times since September it had almost become routine. For the life of me I could not understand why I continued to have blood drawn. I just kept thinking the doctors were still trying to get all eight of the possible donors and recipients to "match," whatever that meant. I made it through Monday and Tuesday by completing all of my grading for my classes. I said my goodbyes and got the phone tree of colleagues lined up for Tom to text them when I was out of surgery. All along I had planned to have my surgery on the 11th, recoup for the remainder of December and the first week in January, and then I would have a good four weeks behind me to go right back to teaching. Well, that was easier said than done.

My plan had also been to spend Wednesday at home getting my condo cleaned up because Mom was coming to help for a few days. Well, that didn't go as planned either. I was required to be at the hospital Wednesday morning for the "pre-surgery" stuff. No one told me about that! Oh, well, we packed up Tuesday night ready to go to the hospital early Wednesday morning.

Greening Out Facebook

After I announced my approval to be a kidney donor on Facebook a few months back, I continued to ask for prayers, gave updates on potential matches, and announced the surgery date. It occurred to me that it would be really cool to get as many friends as we could to "green out" their Facebook page on December 11th. Kelly green is the color for organ donation. So, appropriate, don't ya' think? *Kelly* and *Green*—which IS my favorite color, by the way!

So, earlier in the week Tom and I asked our Facebook friends to "green-out" their pages in honor of organ donation. Amazingly many of them did just that! They not only greened-out their pages, but they either shared my post about donating my kidney or a prayer and some even shared personal stories they had with organ donation in their families. We didn't crash Facebook with our green-out initiative, but we had fun watching everyone green-out their pages, spread the word about living organ donation, and that felt really good. This was just another sign that what I was doing had purpose and with it, we all can have an impact on His Kingdom.

No Room in the Inn

We arrived at the admitting area around 9:00 AM, checked in and waited, and waited some more. Evidently there were no rooms ready for me yet, nor anyone else in the waiting room. I mistakenly left my phone in the car and seriously thought I was having withdrawals! I needed my phone! Okay, so I didn't "need" it, but you know what I mean.

I did have my computer, so I was able to post things and talk to a few people via email. I was afraid if Tom went to get my phone they would call us back to a room, so he held off for a while. I tried to see it as another test of patience. I did not get to this place in the blink of an eye, so what were a few more hours.

Tom would text family to let them know what was happening. He eventually went back to the car to retrieve my phone so I really wasn't deprived for that long. Getting a room, however, was another story. I don't remember how many hours we sat there, but it was H-O-U-R-S!

As we talked through the logistics of what we thought the next few days held for both of us, we noticed a couple sitting in the corner directly across the room from us. Just like I created stories about the ladies having mammograms a few months back, I started creating stories about this couple.

Were they there as a kidney transplant recipient or could they be donating a kidney? Could one of them be MY recipient? Where were they from? I don't really know why we didn't just get up and ask them, but I assumed the people in the waiting area were not just kidney people waiting on a room, but probably there for all types of surgery, so I believe that's what kept us from asking.

The Healthy Patient

Finally, a room was ready. Hallelujah! I settled in and began to finish addressing my Christmas cards and write my newsletter article for the Alabama Art Educator's Association. Tom got the lay of the land and then went to visit another friend he knew who was in the same hospital.

As I was sitting on my bed, doing all my random stuff, a woman, dressed in street clothes and holding what appeared to be a T-shirt headed straight for my room. There had already been a plethora of people going and coming from the room since we got there, so I had just left the door open. As she got closer, she said my name, and then she said, "I'm Jill." It was UAB Jill! I couldn't believe it! The woman I had corresponded with many, many times over the past 11 months was finally standing right in front of me.

She asked how I was doing and if I was ready for what was going to happen tomorrow and then she handed me the T-shirt she was holding. It was Kelly green with a big yellow Superman-style image on the front. The "S" had been replaced with a "K" and then "Donor" was written across the bottom. How cool was that! I couldn't wait to wear it. It was probably then that I realized this is REALLY about to happen.

We talked for a bit and I told her my version of the Santa Fe story. You remember, the one where I said "Yes" and I thought I had dropped the call? She said she was stunned when I said yes because most people don't go forward in the process. She had her standard, "That's okay. Thank you." speech all ready to say to me and when I said yes, it threw her for a loop. She had to think really fast about what she was supposed to say to someone when they say yes. She wished me well and thanked me again for going forward in the kidney donation process. She said, "We really do think of people like you—donors—as superheroes."

More nurses, interns, and doctors continued to pour in and out of my room all day and night. The only "bad" thing that just about made me stand up, get my things, and run home was sticking me with the IV. Oh, my, goodness! I had dozens of pokes, pricks, and sticks into my veins over the course of the past 7-8 months so I was use to needles. Plus, all of the nurses who took those gazillion vials of blood talked about what great veins I had. I had many surgeries before this one, so I also knew what an IV needle would feel like. It would not be fun, but for the love! They could not get a needle in my arm without my veins collapsing. I have never wanted to scream so loudly in all of my days! It was excruciating!

One nurse tried SIX times to get the needle in and finally gave up. I was told later that most of the time when a nurse can't get a needle in to someone's veins within 2-3 tries, they call for someone else to try. Not this chick! She just kept sticking me! I knew not to wiggle or squirm, but it was all I could do not to shoot straight back into the brick wall behind the bed. Finally, an intern asked if she could try and voila, she did it! Second try, but she did it!

Over the next few days my poor arm looked like I had been in a fight with someone or something that had taken its anger out on my forearm! I was black and blue for over a week.

Along with all the nurses, interns, and doctors who came in that day, one of them just stopped at the foot of the bed and said, "I'm sorry. I don't mean to stare, but we don't see many healthy patients." I was still in my normal clothes sitting on the bed doing work stuff on my computer, so I guess I did look a bit different than most of their patients. Little did I know just how "sick" some people are before they get a second chance at life. Many kidney patients go YEARS on dialysis and other treatments before they ever get a kidney transplant. Some go years and never have a transplant. So, yeah, I looked a lot different than most transplant patients the nurses had seen.

Restless Night/Busy Morning

I tried to sleep as much as one can in a hospital. They cannot leave you alone for more than a few hours before they have to come in, wake you up, just so they can monitor you. So, it was not the best night's sleep I had ever had, but it was some sleep.

Early the next morning, more doctors, interns, and nurses came swarming into my room. The day before had been relatively low-key compared to the morning of December 11th. One doctor came in and marked my right side so they would know which kidney to take, only to have another one come in a little later and do it again. For a little bit, I thought, "Okay, you guys, do you talk to each other? Do you know what the other one is supposed to be doing?" I hoped they were just double-checking so they would only take one of my kidneys and leave everything else in place.

I was wheeled to a holding area where all of my vitals were taken for the hundredth time, any last-minute questions would be answered, the last consultation would be given, and the anesthesia would be administered. As I made small talk with the nurses, Tom was taking pics and relaying to me what was going on with Facebook and texts from friends and family. It was like he was reciting prayers to me as I was getting ready for one of the biggest events in my life. I was calm. I was prepared. I was sure this was what God had asked me to do.

As luck would have it, or maybe God planned for the main nurse taking care of me that day was also a member of our church. That was yet another sign I was in good hands and right where I was supposed to be. I quickly told her my story and she was intrigued and wished me well. The lead surgeon, Dr. Jayme Locke, came in with a team of surgeons to tell me what was about to happen and see if I had any questions.

I had heard that Dr. Locke would often pray with patients before surgery. I knew she was a strong believer because she said she knew matching all the people they had put together so far was no fluke, there was a reason for all of it. We didn't ask her to pray with us, but I wished we had. I could feel her confidence and her peace throughout the room. I knew I was in good hands—her's and His.

As the time drew closer to "put me under," all of my past surgeries started flooding my mind. For all the surgeries I've had throughout my life, I never think about death until just before I go under. I do, however, recall a time when I woke DURING a surgery. Yeah, you read that correctly...DURING surgery. I had one surgery to correct a deviated septum along with rhinoplasty. Heck, while they were in there why not get things straightened out a little! Anyway, from that first surgery one side of my nose collapsed and I had to have a second surgery.

In the middle of the second surgery, I woke up. Weirdest feeling, I think I've ever had. I could hear everything, and I do mean everything, but I couldn't say anything. There was a sheet over my face, and they were obviously working on my nose. Evidently I was able to wiggle a little and the surgeon realized I was awake. He immediately told them to get me back "out" and they did. I've often wondered if that's what it feels like to be in a coma. You can hear everything being said and are cognizant of things around you, but you can't say anything to anyone. Horrible feeling!

I'm not sure why I don't really worry about death until just before I'm put "under". Maybe I realize at that moment something could possibly go wrong and I might not make it back, but at that point there is no turning back. The same thing happened December 11, 2014. Briefly I thought, "Have I told everyone I love them? Have I seen everyone I needed to see? Am I at peace with everything if God decides He wants me home now?" The answer, for most everything, was "Yes." I'm sure there were things I left unsaid I would like to have said, but for the most part I was okay with whatever God decided. He had directed every step in this journey so it was His to complete.

One Less Kidney

Thankfully I don't recall any part of this particular surgery, but I do remember a lot about afterwards. Once I woke in recovery, I said my name, where I was, etc. I answered all the questions they ask to see if your cognizant enough to head back to your room. The recovery area must have been packed that day just like the waiting room the day before because as soon as I passed their "test" I was wheeled on out of there.

I'm not really sure about the timeline of the day, but I do know it was an all-day affair. I started the morning bright and early, laid in the pre-op area for a while, had my surgery, stayed in recovery, and finally was wheeled back to my room sometime later that afternoon.

Tom was there to greet me and kissed me once they got me parked. The nurses said the surgery had gone well, I was doing great, and someone would be in to check on me soon. I'm sure there was more conversation than that, but that's about all I remember of the day. And, I remember thinking, "So, I've got one less kidney and someone else has it."

All of my past surgeries had been necessary in order to repair or fix something. My nose surgery was to repair a deviated septum and to fix my crooked nose. My shoulder surgery was to fix a torn rotator cuff. And my hysterectomy was to take out stuff and to fix my horribly painful monthly periods. So, this kidney transplant surgery was quite different. I had voluntarily agreed to being put under anesthesia, with the risk of my own death, to give a perfectly healthy organ to someone I didn't even know. Yes, yes I did this and now I was coming out of it on the other side with one less kidney.

The afternoon continued with a barrage of nurses and doctors checking on me, looking at my incisions, etc. Tom stayed right by my side as I drifted in and out of sleep. He also contacted family and friends to let them know I was out of surgery and all was well. He also kept updates posted to Facebook so people could know the progress throughout the day.

30 or 31?

December 11 for me was pretty much a wash, but Tom was busy meeting all sorts of folks out in the waiting room. Remember that couple we saw sitting in the waiting area the day before? Well, at least one of my scenarios about them was correct. The woman, Carol, was there to receive a kidney. Tom met her husband, David, along with another gentleman, Nate, and a couple from Florida.

The couple from Florida were there for Nate's wife, Faith, who was donating to someone. Karen, the lady from Florida had given a kidney to Nate just three weeks prior because Faith was not a match to him. Faith had gone ahead in the donation process so Nate could get a kidney. She did what I thought I should have done five months prior.

I know this is a confusing scenario, but it's basically what happened with Donna back in July. When someone agrees to donate on your behalf—giving a kidney to someone they do not know—that helps them locate a match for you while also finding a recipient for your friend or family member.

So, one of us, Faith or me, was there to give the woman from the waiting room, Carol, a kidney, but we didn't know which one.

I vaguely remember Tom telling me about all these people he met in the waiting room, but the details were still fuzzy. He did tell me the couple from Florida wanted to meet me. So, in my drunken state of anesthesia I must have agreed to meet them because they soon appeared at my door.

A few nurses were in our tiny room taking vitals and checking on me when suddenly I felt very nauseous. I blew it off as not eating anything yet and turned to meet the couple standing at my door.

Tom tried to quickly retell his story of how he met them and who they were. I did my best to smile and say hello. The nausea was beginning to rear its ugly head, but still I kept it together.

Karen, the woman who had given a kidney just

three weeks prior came to the side of my bed to introduce herself and ask how I was doing. I do remember thinking she looked great for someone who had the same surgery as I just came out of, so that was a positive. Her energetic personality, the lingering anesthesia, and the nausea that was rumbling deep inside of me made it hard to pay attention to everything she was saying, but then she asked, "So, were you 30 or 31?"

I had no idea what she was talking about. As I was trying to decipher what she was asking this thought ran through my mind, "Lady, I am 50 years old! What are you talking about?" I looked over at Tom and he jumped in saying, "Oh, we don't know." Looking at me he said, "Your surgery or Faith's may have been the 31st surgery in the kidney chain here at UAB Hospital and that one would break the record for the longest chain of any hospital."

Wow! I had heard a little bit about this kidney chain thing, but had no idea I would be part of it, much less possibly help break a record. I guess that news was a little too much for my system to handle, because the nausea caused me to look away for a pan, bucket, cup, anything to vomit into.

As I looked around, Karen immediately knew what was about to happen. She said, "She's nauseated. Can you get her something?" Tom's dumbfounded expression looked like, *"What am I supposed to do?"* Little did I know he really had not experienced hospitals at all in his life, so he didn't know when to jump in and assist. He did find a can for me to hold and eventually use, but I held the nausea back for a few more minutes until Karen and her husband could leave and then everything began to spew.

The pain of vomiting hurts regardless of your circumstances, but vomiting with nothing on your stomach is excruciating. Add abdominal surgery to that and oh, my, goodness!

Nurses eventually came back to check on me only to find me heaving into the can. They clarified the vomiting was a side effect of the anesthesia. Great! This had happened once before when I had a hysterectomy, but obviously, I had forgotten about it. It's sort of like giving birth or getting a tattoo—you tend to forget about the horrible pain once it's over. Prior to the hysterectomy surgery I had not gotten sick from anesthesia and was able to start eating pretty quickly after surgery. Not this time! I wouldn't be eating for a long time!

That afternoon and evening were extremely long and painful. Other friends wanted to come by and see me, but I asked Tom to tell them not to come. I felt bad for not seeing people, but I felt even worse physically. I was in no shape to receive visitors.

Facebook Post

December 12, 2014 (Tom's post)

Good morning everyone. Thank you so much for your prayers and support. The Green Out was a success; many of you changed your profiles or posted organ donation info. As I would read through comments (and yes, I read through almost all of them), it was great to see the questions raised by others who did not understand the reason for it. Thank you! Kelly will be elated when she is able to take it all in.

As for her, she is resting right now. It has been a toss and turn kinda night. She has struggled with nausea (from anesthesia). She has not really been able to eat yet :(Therefore she is still on a pain pump and not pills. Today will not be a day of rest. They plan to remove her catheter, make her walk, poke on her and general check-ups by doctors. We have gotten reports that the recipient is doing well. It is a female, but that is all we know so far. Doctors were very happy with all 4 surgeries yesterday (2 donors, 2 recipients). We have been told that there will be a meet-n-greet on Sat. Please continue to pray for that time. We believe it to be a great opportunity to be a light for Jesus Christ. Thank you again! Tom

THE Day

Saturday was THE day! THE day I was to meet my recipient. THE day I had dreamed about for months. THE day friends and family had been praying for just as many months. Today was THE DAY.

I woke feeling so much better than the day before. All the nausea was gone and I was up eating and going to the restroom by myself. Granted I was moving very slowly, but up and moving nonetheless.

The nurse came in to take out my IV. It came out much easier than it did going in! I was disconnected from all the machines they hook you to keeping track of your vital signs. I even got dressed and put on make-up. I was feeling much better.

In the weeks leading up to the surgery I had day-dreamed about who the recipient might be. Woman or man? Black, white, Hispanic, Asian, etc.? Old or young? It was almost like anticipating the arrival of a baby, especially if you didn't find out what you were having before the baby was born. That anticipation of not knowing was exciting.

One of the many surgeons, doctors, or nurses who were in and out of my room that morning let it slip that my recipient was in fact a woman. Tom picked up on it first and asked, "Oh, so it IS a woman?" The doctor looked like he had just let the cat out of the bag! He quickly said, "Yes, it is a woman even though you're not supposed to know that!"

So, immediately my mind began thinking about what sort of woman. Young or old? Black or white? Her family? How sick had she been? Again, just anticipating the unknown continued to excite me.

Once I had been approved as a donor, we were told as the anonymous living organ donor it would be up to my recipient to choose whether or not they wanted to meet me. We had prayed for someone who needed a kidney and to meet them, but we also had prepared ourselves in case he or she didn't want to meet. As excited as I was to meet him or her, I had to emotionally prepare my heart for this worst-case scenario. Meeting your donor is a very personal decision and I had to be willing to accept their decision. Luckily, my recipient agreed to meet me.

Originally, there were to be eight surgeries on

December 11th - 4 donors and 4 recipients—but, for whatever reason only a total of four surgeries were done that day. The other two surgeries that happened the same day as our surgeries would be meeting each other first and then we would be led into the same room to meet each other. I had prepared a small gift for my recipient, a copy of the *Jesus Calling* devotional, one of the bookmarks like I made for my greeter team, and a short note. I do remember thinking I wanted to tell the person my entire year's crazy story as soon as I met them, but I knew that would be overwhelming and it was not the right time. Hopefully there would be a time to share with them later.

As I headed down the hospital hall to the "meeting room," I felt like Tim Conway's character, The Oldest Man, from *The Carol Burnett Show*, shuffling my way down the hallway. It felt like it took a month to go 30 feet! I wasn't moving very fast, but I was making my way.

I was so nervous! I hadn't really thought through the emotions I might feel when this day finally came. It was always a day I prayed would come, but I had not prepared myself for how I would feel going in to meet him/her. I tried not to let anyone else know how nervous I was by joking about anything to keep

the attention off of my nerves. Inside I was a basket-
case!

As we entered the room, Nate, the gentleman
who received a kidney a few weeks prior, was sitting
at the far end of a big conference room table. The
woman sitting to his right was Carol, the woman we
had seen sitting across from us in the waiting room.
Then Nate's wife, Faith, sat to the right of her. So, I
immediately knew I was probably not involved with
any of those people's surgeries, but I still wasn't
completely sure.

Dr. Locke and some of the other surgeons and
nurses were in the room to greet us and tell me
where to sit. I took my seat as Tom stood behind me.
Nate, Faith, and Carol asked if I was the donor and
if I knew my recipient. I told them I was, but I did
not know who my recipient was. They also clarified
that Nate, the man at the end of the table, had
received a kidney three weeks ago from a woman in
Florida. Ahhhhh, it was all starting to make sense
now! The "woman from Florida" was Karen who
had come to see me the day before. Nate's wife,
Faith, had donated on his behalf to the woman,
Carol, sitting in between them.

As my foggy brain started to weave the pieces of
the story I had only heard bits and pieces about over

the past few days, I saw the nurses leading someone into the room. Could this be the moment I had prayed about? Was this finally the woman God had called me to help 11 months ago? Who was she?

There's Something About Mary

As the doctors directed the woman into the room I could see a blond woman in a grey and white chevron printed robe holding and pushing an IV stand. Behind her, also helping her in, was a tall, thin, dark-haired man, that I assumed was her husband. She didn't look at me initially. She looked around the table like she was trying to take in all of our faces, and like me, she was trying to put the pieces of this puzzle together. As she looked down the table at the couple and the other woman, she asked if one of them was her donor. They all said no and pointed to me.

I was sitting directly across the table from where the doctors sat her and I quickly smiled and said, "It was me." She immediately thanked me from across the table and I got up to walk over to her. As we went to hug each other, I felt the emotions welling up inside me. Finally, all of the tests, all of the hurdles, all of the setbacks, all of the hoops I had to jump through to become an organ donor were made clear in that very moment.

Tears welled up in both of us as we hugged for the first time. We quickly introduced ourselves as Kelly and Mary. Mary. Her name was Mary.

After we settled down from the excitement and relief of meeting each other, Dr. Locke stepped in to say a few things. She said she didn't believe our being there on that day was just a coincidence, there was a higher reason we were all there. She told us how sometimes donors and recipients find common things between them that they never knew or they make connections about things they never knew they had as well.

As she made these comments I looked over at Mary and asked where she was from. She said they were from Huntsville. My only connection to Huntsville was that it is about 45 minutes away from my hometown and several of my high school friends live and work there, so that didn't seem to hold any connection. I found out she is an accountant. She has one child and she was very thankful for what I had done for her family.

One of the most intriguing things of our meeting was when Mary and Carol looked at each other and stated, "Don't you feel so much better?" Usually when people have been so sick with kidney issues they often don't realize how sick they really were until they receive a transplant, then the effect is almost immediate.

Just like the nurse who stared at me because she wasn't used to seeing healthy patients, I'm pretty sure I looked at Mary and Carol the same way. How could they possibly feel better already? That told me their new kidneys must be working okay.

As foggy as my mind was, I do remember just looking around the table in amazement at what God had done. He had orchestrated multiple surgeries within a couple of weeks and I was witnessing three people who were previously very sick and now reaping the benefits of His grace.

I'm not sure how long we actually spent together, but I couldn't stop smiling. After almost 11 months of tests, prayers, discouragement, and many, many challenges I was beyond happy.

Going Home

After we met each other, shared stories, and shed more tears it was time for me to go home. I had been cleared to leave the hospital, but Mary had to stay. Usually the person receiving the kidney has to stay longer to be monitored for several days, or even weeks.

Little did we know that Mary had been in the hospital since the first few days of December. She has polycystic kidney disease and needed to stay in the hospital for several weeks to be monitored. Her medications would need to be adjusted and the kidney would need to be monitored for rejection.

Once I was packed and taken to the parking lot via a wheelchair, I realized I was hungry. Like I was really hungry! Yesterday's day-long vomiting drama was over and I was in need of food. I honestly do not remember the trip home except for the moment when I happened to look up and see Newk's restaurant on the right-hand side of the road. In my still tired, anesthesia-laden brain, I was able to sit up and say, "Newk's!" Tom pulled off the road, pulled into Newk's, and got me my favorite chicken salad sandwich. I wish I could remember the sandwich and the drive home, but all of that is a faint memory. I'm sure it tasted really good.

Temporary Pain

Unfortunately, I began developing a cold a day or so before the surgery. Little did I know; they could have canceled the surgery had I gotten really sick. Yikes!

Once we arrived home I slept a lot while Tom fielded phone calls and text messages, all while checking on me. My mom came a few days later to help out so Tom could continue working without feeling guilty he wasn't at home with me.

I am convinced my mom has already earned her angel wings in heaven due to all the nursing assignments she's been given over the years. She doesn't have a degree in nursing, but she could have. She had taken great care of my sister and me all of our lives. Sure, she's a mom and that was her responsibility, but she's gone above and beyond just "taking care of us." She's helped me with every surgery I've ever had (eight as of this writing), the birth of my kids, and the same for my sister. What makes her a "saintly nurse" is all the surgeries and illnesses she helped my dad through. He jokingly called her "the nurse from hell," but we called her Florence Nightingale.

Mom stuck around for most of that first week helping me get around, fielding more phone calls, and visitors. Our church small groups and other friends brought us meals so Mom and Tom could focus on helping me. They were all God-sends! Not having to worry about cooking, cleaning, or just taking care of daily things allowed me to rest and heal.

Once the anesthesia wore off and the pain came back, I was miserable. Well, maybe miserable is too harsh, but I could feel everything. Every time I tried to roll over in bed or on the couch, I could feel what felt and sounded like my entire insides swishing back and forth in my abdomen. I was beginning to wonder if the doctors had put everything back in its proper place. Between the pain and the bad cold, I was really hurting. The pain from the surgery was tolerable, especially with the great pain medications the doctors sent home with me, but having a chest cold exasperated the pain. I was coughing frequently and with a lot of intensity. Every time I coughed my abdomen would tense and that's where most of the pain came from.

I was slow to get into the bed, and just as slow to get out, but figured out a maneuver of rolling onto my left side, raising my body up on my left elbow, and then pushing with my right arm to get upright in the bed. One day I was waking up and trying to muster enough strength to perform my roll-prop-push move when our cat, Scooter, decided he wanted to cuddle with me and jumped straight onto my stomach. Holy cat! He was probably a good 10 pounds plus, so his pounce felt like someone dropped a 10-pound bowling ball on me. I screamed and scared him so badly he immediately jumped off the bed to the other side. Thankful he didn't tear any of my incisions, even if it felt like he did.

Throughout my entire recovery I only cried once. The roll-prop-push move, although sounding harmless, actually hurt a good bit. Every time I needed to go to the restroom or just get up to walk around, it was an ordeal. One day after rolling, propping, and pushing for what seemed like the hundredth time, I just sat on the edge of the bed and cried. Tom asked if I was okay and of course I told him I was fine I was just hurting really badly. As I got myself together, all I could think of were the looks on Mary and Carol's faces and how they talked about feeling so much better just two days after surgery. God convicted me on the spot telling me this temporary pain was doing a great thing for someone else who had been in pain most of her life. My crying stopped immediately.

Facebook Post

December 16, 2014: I appreciate all the sweet comments, I REALLY do, but I would be remiss if I didn't give God ALL the glory. I not only heard Him remind me that I had 2 kidneys, but that I needed to give Him the credit for working all this out. I would like to think I would have done this on my own, but I honestly can't say. I just know the journey has been amazing and the pain is worth it when I think of Mary and her family and the years they will now spend with each other. I pray others will consider living organ donation, the lives they could extend, and the impact they will have on His kingdom!

THE REST OF THE STORY

*"But don't just listen to God's word. You
must do what it says. Otherwise, you are
only fooling yourselves."*

— JAMES 1:22 (NLT)

Paul Harvey

Some of you reading this will have no clue who Paul Harvey was, but he is known for his famous tagline, "And now you know the rest of the story." He was a legendary radio broadcaster for the ABC Radio Networks from 1952-2008. He told some of the best stories! Harvey had a clever way of cutting away to a commercial and leaving you hanging to hear the rest of the story he was telling.

While most people get up and take a potty break or grab a snack during commercial breaks, Harvey's stories kept people in their seats anxious to hear the conclusion of his intriguing story. I can remember having lunch at my grandparent's house when Paul Harvey's radio program came on. Honestly, I can't recall a specific story, but I do remember his velvety voice and that iconic tagline, "and now you know the rest of the story," intermingled throughout his broadcasts.

So, what does Paul Harvey have to do with this story of organ donation and hearing God's voice? Well, there is even more to this story than just what happened between January and December 2014. Many of the questions and dilemmas I encountered during that year were finally answered or made crystal clear in the months and years following.

One of the most puzzling questions I had throughout this journey was why I couldn't make a decision to go forward in the donation process until the middle of the summer in 2014. That answer came shortly after our surgeries and totally blew me away when I finally heard why. Financial difficulties were a huge part of Tom and my marriage troubles, among other issues, but through changes in attitude, practices, and tithing, we are in the best place financially we've been in a long time. During 2014, our marriage was a struggle at best, but through a lot of prayer, seeking Godly counsel, and some really big changes we found healing and love again. And finally, I believe this entire journey was leading me to write this book, to spread the message of hearing God's voice in our day-to-day lives, and to find my true calling in order to fulfill God's purpose while on this earth. So, now here's the rest of this story.....

Biggest Reveal

Mary continued to stay in the hospital throughout December 2014 and we stayed in touch almost daily. We had the opportunity to participate in a news conference held at UAB Hospital to announce the recent record-breaking surgeries for the kidney chain. The woman who started the chain, Paula King, spoke about her willingness to donate and how others should consider donating because of the number of people on the transplant waiting list. (As of this writing there are over 116,000 people on waiting lists around the United States.)

Mary was asked to speak at the news conference

and more of the pieces of her story started to come together. She shared she has polycystic kidney disease. Her mother had it and died from it. Because of this she had to have a living organ donor for her particular situation.

Shortly after the news conference was over, one of the television stations asked Mary and me to share our feelings about our surgeries. Mary shared that I was her "angel" and she was so thankful for my willingness to donate a kidney to a stranger. She had no idea what I had been through over the past year, but I was even more clueless as to what she and her family had been going through for years.

Mary was not confined to a bed the whole time she remained at UAB Hospital, so Ann-Ashton and I decided to get her out for a little while and have lunch at a local restaurant. Her daughter happened to be in town and went with us.

We picked Mary and her daughter up at the condominiums located close to the hospital. The condos are owned by the hospital for patients, like Mary, who need to stay close for observation and testing, but do not necessarily need to stay in the hospital.

As we enjoyed our lunch we also began to share our stories of how we came to be a donor and recipient. I shared my story of trying to help Donna get a kidney, how we were not a match, but she did receive a kidney, and how I decided to keep going in the process. I didn't really tell her the nitty-gritty details of how I felt God leading me to do this or all the craziness I had gone through over the year, but I gave her the highlights.

She explained a little more about her polycystic kidney disease and why she had to have a living kidney donor. The disease is hereditary, but they have not determined if her daughter has it or not. Although Mary knew most of her life that she had the disease, she did not really suffer with it until after the birth of her daughter. At the time of Mary's surgery, her daughter was a pre-teen, so Mary's health had gotten progressively worse for the past 11-12 years.

As she began to share her story I couldn't help but be moved by how her illness had impacted her entire family. She was never on dialysis, but she was getting close. She said she basically drug herself out of bed every morning, made it through the work day, went straight home, and fell asleep. Her quality of life was obviously poor and getting worse by the day.

I also found out why I had to undergo what seemed like endless blood tests. Mary had high antibodies in her blood and the doctors continued testing our blood together to see if they would be compatible. The doctors would "dilute" her blood and then check it to see how it played with my blood.

Because she was not on dialysis yet, those blood tests/comparisons allowed the doctors to estimate the number of plasmapheresis treatments she would undergo before the surgery in order for our blood to work together. Plasmapheresis is similar to dialysis, but is a process where the liquid part of the blood, or plasma, is separated from the blood cells. The plasma is then replaced with another solution such as saline, or the plasma is treated and then returned to the patient's body.

She had been on Vanderbilt Hospital's waiting list for over a year when she came to UAB Hospital. By that time, she was very sick and getting weaker every day. Her husband told us he had watched her struggle to get through a normal day and it was getting to the point she couldn't attend their daughter's sporting events. Mary's health and their family's day-to-day activities were all suffering the longer she went without receiving a kidney.

Then, she said THE most amazing thing to me. As Mary continued to share her journey of getting to UAB Hospital she slipped in a quick statement that just about blew me off my chair. She said, "Yeah, we didn't come to UAB until late July."

Wait, what did she say? I'm not sure if my face showed the astonishment I was feeling, but my soul was stirred beyond belief!

I'm not sure if you caught that either, but Mary didn't even make the trip to Birmingham to see if doctors at UAB Hospital could help her until late JULY! Remember when I FINALLY made my decision to go forward in the donation process? J-U-L-Y!!!!!!

That moment felt like when you're having your eyes checked, and the doctor puts that big contraption in front of your face with different lenses making it impossible to see. You know the one? The doctor asks which one is better, "1 or 2? 2 or 3?" and so on. Then, based on your answers, they finally put two lenses together that allow you to see everything perfectly. It was the same feeling when Mary announced when she came to UAB Hospital. All of a sudden the struggles, the indecision, the doubting I had felt over the past year all came into perfect focus.

God had orchestrated the timing for both of us in July 2014. He led Mary to finally seek other medical help when she was at her sickest and He held back my decision to go forward in the donation process until He got her to UAB Hospital. Thankfully I listened and didn't decide to stop my role in the donation process.

Ann-Ashton and I enjoyed our time getting to know Mary and her daughter but I honestly cannot tell you anything else that was said that afternoon. I was in awe of what God had been up to even when I didn't think He was listening to my prayers.

Financial Blessings

After my surgery and impending recovery, Tom and I were blessed beyond our wildest dreams. The first blessing came in the form of an unexpected Christmas gift.

I spent the first week after surgery sleeping and trying to heal. As the following Sunday rolled around Tom's usher team was scheduled to serve, so he went to church while I watched the service online. When he returned home, he reported on everyone he saw, relayed all their well-wishes, and explained how he fielded all their questions. While telling me all of this, he handed me a small box wrapped in Christmas paper. I asked who it was from and he said he didn't know. He said my co-leader, Lee, had given it to him to give to me. I pushed further about who gave it to her. He again said he honestly didn't know.

People had visited all week bringing us meals and checking on me. We still had plenty of food left over, so Tom proceeded to finish telling me about who he had seen at church, while preparing lunch. As I unwrapped the Christmas paper, I continued to question who it was from. Tom finally said, "Well, Lee said she stepped out of the team meeting room for just a minute and when she came back in, there was the package. I don't know if she even knows who sent it."

The box was an old Cingular cell phone box. Wow, that brought back memories from the early 2000s! It had a little weight to it, so I was confused at what might be inside. I opened one end of the box and saw what looked like thin cardboard pieces stacked one on top of the other. As I pulled the rest of the flaps of the box open, I saw it was actually dollar bills stacked one on top of the other and the box was packed FULL!

I was speechless! Tears began welling up in my eyes as I tried to call for Tom. He was still getting food ready and talking, but he finally looked over at me sitting on the sofa. Between fighting back tears and trying to speak, I said, "It's full of cash." He immediately choked up and ran over to see for himself.

We cried and looked high and low for a name, a card, anything, but found none. We did find one of our church's "Acts of Kindness" cards, but there was no name on it. Our church supplies us with cards, about the size of a business card, that simply say "Something Extra to Show You God Loves You." Tom and I had given out several of these cards before, but never imagined we would be the benefactors of one and certainly not one this large.

It was no *little* act of kindness, there was a total of $1,700 packed into that little box! We were dumbfounded and overwhelmed. It took us a while to comprehend what had happened. I had been worrying about how we were going to provide Christmas for the kids that year, so the anonymous gift was certainly an answer to a prayer.

After I calmed down and got my wits about me, I called Lee. I tried to get her to admit who gave us the gift. I really thought it was her and the team, and maybe still believe it could have been, but she swore up and down it was not her. She did seem genuinely surprised when I told her what was in the box.

Regardless of who sent the gift, we were beyond thankful.

This unexpected blessing came along at the perfect time and taught me a valuable lesson of trusting God when we find ourselves in a financial conundrum. Tom is much better at this than me. I need assurance there is money in the bank and we're financially okay. We both work hard and we have a steady income, but he always trusts the Lord will provide when we are in a tight.

For the next 6 months or so we tried a lot of different things to help with our financial issues. We consulted with financial coaches at the church to help us understand how to handle the money we did have and plan for future income. One of the advisors looked at all of our financials and said, "On paper, there is no way you all are making it!" She told us we really were living on a wing and a prayer, and she was right. Since 2014, God has continued to bless us with people and money coming from places we never imagined.

In the summer of 2015 Tom and I were helping with the church's GROW conference. GROW is an annual conference bringing pastors from all over the world to Birmingham to learn from Church of the Highlands how to grow their own churches. Tom worked with the usher team and helped with some of the logistics of the conference. I was helping behind the scenes with snacks and drinks for the Dream Teamers serving at the conference.

During some of the down time at the conference, I spotted a friend, Karan, who I had not seen in several years also helping with the conference. We quickly caught up about what was going on with our families and somewhere in our conversation I shared how we were struggling with money issues. She and her husband had also been financial counselors at the church and she offered me some advice. The one nugget of information I took away from our chat was a book she recommended. She suggested Robert Morris' book *The Blessed Life* and told me it "totally changed her thoughts on tithing and handling money based on Biblical principles."

Karan's enthusiastic endorsement of the book had me sold. I went home and ordered a copy. She was right, the book totally changed my thinking about money. After reading it, I immediately changed our monthly tithe to 10% of our income. I knew the amount would strap our budget a bit more and we didn't have much margin in our finances as it was, but felt compelled to get our finances prioritized in the way God expects them to be.

Later that summer I started a part-time job at a local Michaels' store. Our finances still weren't where we needed them to be, so I felt a part-time job might help supplement a bit more. Tom was working just about any job people would pay him to do. So, once again, our marriage was being strained. We were working apart Monday through Thursday, and then separately over the weekends. We were exhausted, anxious, and on edge with each other. I even contacted a bankruptcy attorney in desperation to "fix" our financial situation.

Working on Our Marriage

The beginning of February 2015 started with a counseling session with the pastor who married us a little over three years prior. As hard as it was for us to confess we needed counseling, we swallowed our pride and started talking.

We realized our living arrangements (me living in another town four days out of the week), our financial situation, and our parenting/step-parenting styles were putting a huge strain on our marriage. Maybe just talking to another person we held in high regards allowed us to talk more freely.

After hearing both sides of our story and after

sharing our huge argument back in December, he told us three things that seemed so simple, but made so much sense.

1-Get right with the Lord

2-Learn something we don't know about parenting/step-parenting

3-Develop a plan for our lives and then rehearse the plan

Like I said, these seems so simple *now,* but at the time we couldn't see the forest for the trees! It took Godly counsel from good friends who weren't afraid to talk honestly and openly with us and to seek professional counseling to reveal God's truths in our lives.

Devil in the Distraction

Valentine's Day fell on a Saturday in 2015, so Tom decided to surprise me Thursday, February 12 when I arrived home with a Valentine's dinner at J. Alexander's. Surprisingly, we had to wait over a half-hour to get a table. Evidently everyone had the same idea Tom had to go to dinner Thursday instead of over the weekend. Plus, Friday was the 13th so who wants to go out for dinner on Friday the 13th?

Tom and I talked a lot that night, while waiting

for a table and all through dinner. It was probably
one of the best conversations we'd had in a long time.
He was getting a lot more work and my job was
going well. I was helping to lead a church small
group in Troy and he was getting more plugged in
with the guys in his small group.

I remember asking Tom why he thought God
would show favor to both of us at the same time, but
in different places? I now realize it was NOT God
showing us favor. It was actually the Enemy
continuing to separate us.

Later, I found a quote by Deric Muhammad that
smacked me right in the face solidifying that very
thought. "When the enemy cannot destroy you, his
job is to DISTRACT you." He was distracting us
then and has continued to distracted us from time to
time ever since then.

Another Revelation

Knowing Ann-Ashton had been accepted to Troy
University for the fall of 2016 I knew my housing
situation in Troy would have to change. I tried to talk
to Tom about how we might be able to rent an
apartment or house in Troy, but the conversations
didn't get very far. I knew there was really no way

we could afford another big expense like renting an apartment while maintaining mortgage payments on our condo at the same time. Then, in October of 2015, everything changed.

I walked into our condo late one Thursday after teaching and driving two hours from Troy. Tom was sitting on the couch and I went over to kiss him and then talk about our week like I did most Thursday evenings. After a little small talk, Tom nonchalantly announced he was closing his business in the coming weeks and we were moving to Troy. Huh, say what? I was dumbfounded!

Remember, Tom had started his construction business at the same time I was starting my new job at Troy University, so I never imagined he would move to Troy. I had thought it might be a possibility somewhere down the road, but never imagined he would decide to do it on his own.

Fast forward a few months and we had our condo on the market, began house hunting in Troy, and started selling as much of our stuff as we could. Surprisingly, by January 2016, the condo sold in less than a month and Tom landed a job in Troy. We "officially" moved to Troy the first of February 2016 but with no place to live. We had to wait for the condo sale to close before we could purchase a house in Troy, so my boss offered us her fifth-wheel camper. From the first part of February until the last day of March Tom, our chocolate lab Lucy, and I lived in the camper. I always thought I would love to live in a "tiny house," but that experience changed my mind.

We've now lived in Troy for a little over two years and I can happily report that it has saved our marriage. Tom later admitted that his decision to move us to Troy was in fact to save our marriage. I am forever grateful for that selfless act of love and devotion he demonstrated then and continues to do every day. We still miss the city, our friends, and our church, but we go back to visit as often as we can.

Another bright moment in this fledgling marriage and financial disaster story was the fact that moving to Troy not only saved our marriage, but because the cost of living is so much cheaper and Tom landed a job with a weekly salary, we were able to pay off our credit card consolidation with *GreenPath Financial Wellness* a year earlier than expected. We're not completely out of the woods yet, but we're making progress on paying down our debt, increasing our tithe to the church, and we've been able to help others every now and then just like we were blessed only a few years back.

The anxiety of basically living week-to-week was making me a little crazy. But now that we are tithing every month, paying down bills, and budgeting more wisely, life is much less stressful.

How Do You Know?

Another surprise that came in January 2015 was when my dad asked me to speak to his and Mom's Sunday School class about my kidney donation. First, I was a bit shocked he wanted me to share my story with his Sunday School class. I'm not sure why, but I think it told me he and I were finally okay. We would never see eye-to-eye on some things, but his request showed me he was proud of me. He might never say the words, but his actions spoke volumes.

I was a bit anxious speaking at my parents' church, not because it was their church or because it was also the church where I grew up, but because the last time I spoke at the church I was 15 or 16 years old and scared to death. I had never spoken in front of a group of people—EVER. I had every word I planned to say written on pieces of notebook paper and I know the back row of the sanctuary could hear the papers shaking in my hands. I was so nervous and I felt like everyone could see it.

I prayed for God to bless my message and to use me like He used Moses. Even with all my speaking opportunities in front of people since becoming a teacher, I was and am still self-conscious about my Southern accent and rather deep sounding voice. In Exodus 4:10 Moses thought his "slow speech and tongue" would keep him from relaying God's message. Then, God came back with, "Who gave human beings their mouths? Who makes them deaf or mute? Who gives them sight or makes them blind? Is it not I, the LORD? Now go; I will help you speak and will teach you what to say" (Exodus 4:11-12 NIV). After reading that, I said, "Okay, God, please tell me what to say!"

As I shared my kidney donation story with Mom and Dad's Sunday School class I felt comfortable and confident. I was not the same speaker I was at 16. The class welcomed me with open arms and invited another class to join them, so I had a packed house! They asked questions about my recipient, my recovery, and they even asked Tom what he thought about all of this. He restated his reluctance to go against God telling me to donate.

While I felt like I was home free and my talk to redeem myself as a speaker at my home church was coming to an end, Dad decided to throw me a curve ball—and a big one. With all the questions about the surgeries and recovery, Dad decided to ask me this question, "So, you talk about *hearing from God,* but how do you know it's really Him?"

I was again dumbfounded. Did he really just ask me *that* question?

Although I was taken aback, I'm not really sure why. Thinking about it now, I guess I assumed everyone would believe me when I said I heard God telling me to donate a kidney. Most everyone I shared my story with were believers, so why wouldn't others believe me? The thought of someone doubting my story was beyond my realm of reasoning, so why was Dad asking me this now?

Ironically, looking back through my journal from January 2015 I wrote:

> *January 22, 2015 Devotional from Jesus Calling: Trust Him —anything that makes me anxious is a* **growth opportunity***—don't waste energy regretting things. *How do I know God told me to do this? He interrupted me, and I took the time to finally listen.*

I had actually thought about what I would say if

someone asked me that very question! Evidently, I didn't think it would be my own father!

I quickly assessed my answer and told him it was a feeling I had that wouldn't let go of me and that I continued to feel compelled to go forward. Probably not the best answer, and not the answer I had prepared, but it was what I came up with on the spot. It seemed to satisfy him, and I concluded my talk by thanking the class for having me.

Tom and I talked about the presentation on our way home later that day and I asked him what he thought about Dad's question. He had been taken aback as well. He thought about it and was hoping I would have mentioned my "personal relationship" with God and because of that I could discern what was God's voice and what wasn't.

Well, I missed that opportunity with my dad, but it was a good lesson to learn. Whenever I've been asked that question, or one similar, I always talk about my personal relationship with God, my prayer life, and how I've learned to discriminate what I believe is truly God speaking to me.

Not only do I have a "feeling" God's speaking to me, but I have several safeguards in place to insure if it is His voice or it isn't. One of the first signs I look for is being aware of my circumstances. There are times when I tend to pray, but not listen, so I try to stop while praying to actually listen to what God is saying. If we're doing all the talking, there is no way to hear what the other side is saying!

The next safeguard is thoughts of doing something or feeling expectant that something is happening. While I'm *listening* to God, He may lead me to either take action myself or He might prompt me to seek out others for help. Usually if I'm aware of what's going on around me and I'm listening to God's direction for my life I will also feel like I'm getting information overload. It's like the Holy Spirit is sending me information faster than I can comprehend or write it all down! Hence, the reason I carry a journal with me at ALL times!

Next, whether or not what I *think* God is saying to me is crystal clear or a bit murky, I seek God's Word for clarification. I love the Open Bible app for locating topics I'm interested in or for finding topics I believe God is wanting me to know more about. Seeking answers, ones that do and ones that don't line up with God's will, is just another way of ensuring it is God's will for my life.

Lastly, another precaution I use is seeking Godly counsel. Don't get this wrong, the Bible is THE answer, but if I'm still not completely sure it's God speaking to me I talk to people I trust to give it to me straight. I love author Dallas Willard's comment about this in his book *Hearing God*. He says, "It is God's will that we ourselves should have a great part in determining our path through life." God may be "guiding" me toward a decision He hopes I will make by directing me to other believers.

I've also learned that if God always "fixed" our dilemmas every time we asked, we would never learn to make decisions on our own, we would never learn from our mistakes, and we wouldn't learn to lean on Him for guidance in every area of our lives. We would live in a continuous state of blunder. How could we truly understand His plan for our lives if He's always fixing our messes? How could we make changes in our lives in order to stop making careless mistakes if He fixed it all? Seeking the Bible and Godly counsel puts us in relationship with other believers, but more importantly, it ensures a *relationship with and dependence on Him.*

Lesson learned!

The following month, I was talking to Mom and she shared noticing some changes in Dad. Not necessarily physical changes, but spiritual ones. Dad made a substantial donation to the local cancer center where he had gone for treatments and help throughout the past year. Mom asked him what gave him the idea to make the donation? She asked if he thought it might be God telling him to do it? He said he didn't know, but maybe. *Maybe!* Although *maybe* doesn't sound very convincing, it was actually HUGE for my dad to admit that maybe he heard, felt, or thought God wanted him to give back to a place that had helped him so much. Wow! *Maybe* my story of hearing from God had done something to his heart. Just maybe!

Dad's Next Chapter

Dad had several radiation treatments in January and February of 2015, and then surgery to implant radioactive seeds for combating his prostate cancer in late March. We all hoped this procedure would do the trick and that he would be healed of cancer.

The procedure went as well as could be expected, but life after that was not what anyone could have predicted. He struggled with bleeding, having to self-catheterize, and basically another year of his health slowly declining. The doctors later told Mom that due to Dad's plethora of other health issues, he was one of the few that the side-effects of this procedure were worse than the cancer itself.

After a year of ups and downs, Dad passed away in his sleep on January 14, 2016. His death hit us all very hard. He told us at Christmas in 2015 that he wouldn't be here the next year. Those words were so difficult to hear and to understand, but we wonder if he knew something none of us were privy to, or at least not yet.

Leading Me to Something More

In January 2015, I still had a few weeks before I had to go back to work, but the urge to write began to enter my mind again. I had no idea what I was supposed to write, but I was willing to listen to what God had in mind. Remember back in 2013 during the Super Bowl game, when I felt God speaking to Tom and me about writing a blog? Well, like I said, I don't think Tom ever thought about it again, but I began to seriously think about it. Ads began showing up in my Facebook feed about self-publishing and writing. Unsolicited emails began to appear in my email account about free trainings for starting a blog. Funny how God can even use modern technology to get our attention!

I still wasn't ready to commit to writing anything. Heck, I was only in my fourth semester of teaching at a new job, so starting something "new" was not on my agenda. I had been there and done something very new over the past year, so I thought I was due a bit of "down time" before I had another "new" adventure.

On the way back to Troy after my surgery, I heard God tell me, "You need to listen better, trust more, act quicker, prepare earlier, and "but" less." This time I was not interrupted, so I felt like He was speaking directly to me about where I was heading next. That "but less" statement was telling me I shouldn't say, "I believe God wants me to do....BUT, I'm not sure I have time." In other words, I didn't need to second-guess or make excuses about what God was saying to me.

February and March allowed me to stay busy with work and no real dramas to side-track me. I wrote out Tom and my prayers in great detail during the first quarter of 2015. My writings look like I was desperate to hear again from God, while trying to *get back to normal*. 2014 had rocked my world and I wasn't sure I could go back to "normal" any time soon.

A year as intense and focused as 2014 cannot be sustained for long periods of time and I knew that. I thrive on a challenge and the kidney donation experience was definitely the biggest challenge I had faced in my life. I really wasn't sure I could top that one!

I continued to pray diligently, pursue books, websites, and the Bible for knowledge about my life's purpose and where to go next. The urge to write was still eating at me, but I wasn't sure what that should look like just yet. I continued to find authors, bloggers, and leaders whose stories and platforms encouraged me to keep pursuing God with everything I had.

When I ran across blogger and author Jen Hatmaker's books and blog one day in mid-March, I journaled about her and other women I had come to admire.

Journal Entry: When I see other women speaking and sharing their stories, I think, "What makes me different? Why would anyone want to hear my story? Then I remember my kidney story, and think He led me through all of that for a reason! Maybe I should do something with it!"

As much as I relished reading and finding out about other women's journeys I still wasn't convinced my story would be worth writing about and I doubted others would want to hear about them

anyway. The Enemy was still lurking around in
my head!

So Glad You Listened

The last few weeks in March I was headed west to
New Orleans for the National Art Education
Association's annual convention. As much as I loved
leading the art teachers of Alabama and being part of
the national art educators' research leadership, I was
feeling that tug again to do something different.

Granted I've never felt "content" with just doing
the same thing day after day. I've always felt like
there was more for me to do. I rarely stayed at one
job for more than a year or two until I became an art
teacher. When I started teaching it was like all of my
life's experiences and skills came together at just the
right moment. In 2015 I had been in the same
profession for 19 years and the same school for 14 of
those years. I had finally found my niche, I was
pretty good at it, and truly enjoyed going to work
every day. I had landed my dream job at the
university level, and I assumed this was where I
would retire—and I still do.

I was getting antsy with life again, but this time I
didn't have the plan; someone else did.

I arrived in New Orleans ready to see my art teacher friends from around the country and to serve the last of my responsibilities as the Alabama President and the Elementary Chair on the NAEA Research Commission. One of those art teacher friends, Lisa, and I met 7 years prior at a NAEA event in Maine. Lisa was not someone I initially thought I would "click" with. She's extremely energetic, a little outspoken, and has a heart of gold.

We had not seen each other in a few years so we decided to meet for dinner at a local seafood restaurant. It was so good to see her smiling face and peppy energy. She treated me to a few drinks and a great meal. After we caught up with each other and our families, she said something that stopped me in my tracks. She said, "Girl, I just want to tell you, I am so proud of you for listening!"

She was glad I listened!

She probably doesn't know how significant that statement was to me, but it meant the world. It was yet another sign God had guided my steps and thankfully I had listened to Him. It was also another sign people believed me when I said, "God told me to donate a kidney to a stranger." The ability to say those words without hesitation were getting a little easier to say each time I said them.

The Birth of a Blog

April 5th stood out to me that year, not only because it was my sister's birthday and Easter, but it was the day I decided I would start my blog.

What? Start a blog? Why now?

I'm not sure why "now," but in my journal, I wrote:

Thinking about starting a blog! Trying to get the ball rolling on what I believe God wants me to do towards serving Him through my life. Need a domain name????

Healing Hearts with Art (name I had used back in 2011 with tornado disaster relief) - name is already taken! Ugh!

Finally Listened

When I Listen

When I Listened

When We Listen

Bingo! *When We Listen.* That's it! It's not just when "I" listen, although that's where the idea for the name came from, but when WE listen sounded more inclusive. *When we listen,* He does great things!

Just like the idea for the *Healing Hearts with Art* group in 2011 and when I felt God telling me to donate a kidney, the Holy Spirit took hold of me about starting a blog and it would not let me go.

On my way back to Troy one Monday, I stopped at one of my usual rest stops, Zaxby's restaurant, and heard myself asking the following questions:

What do I do? What am I gifted with being able to do? (Creative, teach, talk, pray, positive energy, helping women, helping children, writing) How can I make a living doing these things? How can I advance His Kingdom by doing these things?

If I could find a way to combine all of these so-called talents AND grow God's Kingdom, I might have found my calling in this world! That was the first time in my adult life that I truly felt like I had a purpose.

I now believe we all have the *same earthly purpose* which is to grow God's Kingdom, but we all have *different gifts and talents* of which we use on a daily basis to fulfill that purpose.

In the following months, I set out to learn everything I could about blogging. I read every blog post I could find that had something to do with blogging, both faith-based and secular. After almost three months of studying and researching the world of blogging, I decided my birthday, June 4th, would become my blog launch day. I always seem

to work harder and better when I know I have a
deadline!

Manna from Heaven

Over the next year and a half people began
appearing in my life, sort of like God miraculously
giving manna to the Israelites exiting Egypt, that
continually affirmed my belief God was indeed
leading my life's steps. One of our graphic design
students found out I was trying to start a blog and
offered to design my logo....for FREE! When I told
him I really couldn't pay him, he said, "That's okay.
This is my gifting! Let me do this for you!"

Then through mutual friends I found a
photographer with a childhood friend who had gone
through a heart transplant, so she offered to take my
initial blog photos....for FREE!

I felt God continually blessing me with other
believers who had their own set of gifts and offers to
help me get this crazy dream off the ground. These
people modeled selflessness through the gifts God
has blessed them with.

Other folks, like the editor of this manuscript,
the book designer, and cover designer, have
continued to pop into my life when God knows they

have talents I do not have and help me with writing, blogging, or anything else I feel led to do. Since moving to Troy I've had the pleasure of meeting two other links in the UAB Kidney Chain, one living here in Troy and another at a women's conference where I shared my testimony about hearing from God.

One of the craziest connections came from Tom meeting a guy in a bar. Sounds like a bad joke, doesn't it?

While we were in the process of selling our condo and moving to Troy back in 2016, Tom was still finishing a few jobs in Birmingham on the weekends. In early March college basketball was gearing up for March Madness and let's just say Tom is a HUGE North Carolina Tarheels fan and was ready to see what his Heels might do that year. North Carolina's biggest in-state rival is the Duke Blue Devils, so Tom naturally wanted to watch their last game of the regular season.

Because we had already disconnected our cable at the condo, there was no way for him to watch the game at home so he decided to go to a local sports bar for dinner and watch the game. Tom is a teetotaler so for him to seek out a bar to go to would have to be for food and access to a television.

As he tells this part of the story, he walked in, saw a guy with a Tarheels' cap on and thought, "Okay, he can't be too bad. He's wearing a Tarheels' cap. I'll go sit by him." To make this part of the story a bit shorter, Tom and the guy, Chris, struck up a great conversation, watched their Heels beat the Duke Blue Devils 76-72, and promised to stay in touch.

Chris shared that he and his wife were building a new house, so he asked Tom for builder advice and Tom graciously offered his two-cents worth and a promise to take a look at their property the next time he was in town. And so, the bromance began.

Over the next few weeks Tom and Chris continued to stay in touch chatting about the Tarheels and the construction of Chris' new house. Somewhere in all of these updates I asked Tom, "So what does Chris do for a living?" I felt like he had already shared this with me, but I obviously wasn't paying very close attention because this time when Tom answered me with, "He's a nurse anesthetist at UAB Hospital," I said, "Whoa! What did you just say?" Tom repeated, "He's a nurse anesthetist at UAB Hospital." This time I stopped what I was doing and said, "You know that's what Ann-Ashton is considering as a nursing career? Do you think he would let her shadow him so she can see what they really do on a daily basis?" Tom said he felt sure Chris would and he would text him to ask.

Fast forward to April when Tom, Ann-Ashton, and I were attending the UAB Hospital's Celebrate Life Picnic in Birmingham. UAB Hospital hosts a large gathering for all organ transplant donors and recipients each year in April. It's a beautiful celebration of people who have given life through living or deceased organ donation to others desperate for a second chance at a full life.

Tom had asked Chris to join us at the picnic and he agreed to come and bring his family. In the time he and Tom had met and gotten to know each other, Chris shared that he knew Dr. Locke (the surgeon who had transplanted my kidney into Mary's body) and had been involved in some of the kidney surgeries. He also shared she was a graduate of Duke and a huge Blue Devils fan. They had a "friendly" Duke/North Carolina rivalry of their own going on in the operating room. Interesting!

Before Chris and his family arrived at the picnic, Tom, Ann-Ashton, and I spotted Dr. Locke and went over to speak to her. Tom and she talked about knowing Chris and their shared interest in Tarheel basketball. Dr. Locke is not only a Duke graduate she also knows her basketball! After some friendly basketball banter, Dr. Locke asked Ann-Ashton if she was in high school or college. Ann-Ashton shared she was a senior in high school and would be attending Troy University in the fall to study nursing. This sparked Dr. Locke to ask her what type of nursing did she think she would like to pursue and Ann-Ashton shared that she was thinking about anesthetics, but wasn't completely sure. Dr. Locke's assistant was standing there with us and told Ann-Ashton if she ever wanted to shadow someone in the kidney transplant area they would set it up for her. Ann-Ashton thanked her and got her telephone information.

As we walked away from Dr. Locke and her assistant I tried not to act too excited, but mouthed "Wow!" to Ann-Ashton. She asked, "Why are you saying 'wow'? Who was that?" I was about to burst! I told her Dr. Locke is one of the driving forces responsible for the success of the kidney donation program at UAB Hospital and for her to offer Ann-Ashton pretty much an open invitation to see what nurses do in that area of the hospital was HUGE!

Chris, or Nurse Chris as I had started to call him, and his family had arrived at the picnic so we set off to locate them in the crowd of donors, recipients, and their families. He had agreed to allow Ann-Ashton to shadow him, but they had yet to connect about a specific time, so we were hoping meeting him face-to-face would allow them time to talk about a possible date.

Tom introduced us to Nurse Chris and we continued to talk to him about Dr. Locke, the Kidney Chain, and all things involved with a kidney surgery. In the midst of talking to him about Dr. Locke and the Kidney Chain Nurse Chris said, "I don't know patient's names and really don't remember faces since I'm usually putting them to sleep, but I do remember Dr. Locke asking me to be in on a surgery that she said was the 'record breaker.' I about fell over, again! Seriously? Could this man, who from all accounts seemed like a "random" guy that Tom met in a bar a little over a year after my kidney surgery be THE nurse involved with our surgeries? No way! Yes, way! We think he was involved with Mary's surgery. Nurse Chris was with Dr. Locke, so we know she was not my main surgeon but the surgeon who had placed my kidney into Mary.

I literally could not stop smiling! Just like when Mary told me she had not gone to UAB Hospital until July of 2014, I was dumbfounded at the orchestration of this whole journey. Again, I quietly said a little prayer, "Wow, God! You continue to amaze me!"

Ann-Ashton went on to shadow Nurse Chris later that summer and was blown away at the access being with him allowed her and amazed at all the interesting surgeries she witnessed. That one day walking alongside one of God's strategically placed angels solidified her resolve to do whatever she needed to do to get into nursing school. As of this writing she has applied for nursing school at Troy University and seems poised at fulfilling her dream.

Still Amazed

After remembering all the intimate details of this journey, I still stand amazed at what God did with me and what He continues to do through others He places in my path. These are just some of the people I recall because of their profound impact on this journey I'm still taking. I have to wonder how many more there were? These are the people I noticed, but what about the ones I missed?

I sincerely believe God puts us on paths that not only show us the love and service of others, but for us to reciprocate that love and service to people we cross paths with every day. It's our job to pay attention and recognize them and to not let missed opportunities pass us by.

Luckily this story about hearing from God allowed me to hear and act on one of those opportunities. There were a lot of "what ifs" scenarios along the way, but looking back I'm thankful I didn't necessarily act on those possibilities. I say that because many of the "what ifs" I've recounted would probably not have resulted in this story having the same sort of ending or emotional impact.

I would probably have taken things into my own hands, and I just don't feel like the story would have ended the same nor would it have been as powerful as the one I've written about here. In the middle of writing it, I often had to stop and remind myself that these things really did happen to me.

Writing the story in a way that others could follow and grasp the powerful components to it was emotionally draining at times. I found myself having to stop and cry for a little while or put the manuscript away for days, even weeks, before I could start writing again. I still pray this journey will touch a heart that might be prompted to become a living organ donor to someone in need, mark "organ donor" on their driver's license, or simply take a moment and learn to truly listen for God's voice speaking words of grace and purpose into their lives.

If God can use a middle-aged, Southern creative with a deep voice to share His story of grace and direction, then He can do anything! My prayer for anyone who takes the time to read my story is they will be inspired to stop....pray....and truly listen to what God speaks into their lives. Get ready, it's probably going to be a wild ride!

So, now you know the rest of the story.

ABOUT THE AUTHOR

KELLY C. BERWAGER, PH.D. is an awarding winning visual art specialist teaching P-16 students for over 20 years. After her year of learning to hear God's voice more clearly, she began to write about her faith, speak at women's events, and conduct art workshops. Kelly helps women of all ages and backgrounds hear God's calling on their lives through artistic endeavors.

WWW.KELLYBERWAGER.COM